Animal Antics

2012

Edited by
Jenni Bannister

First published in Great Britain in 2012 by:
Forward Poetry
Remus House
Coltsfoot Drive
Peterborough
PE2 9BF
Telephone: 01733 890099
Website: www.forwardpoetry.co.uk

Foreword

Animal Antics 2012 sees the return of one of our most popular recurring themes here at Forward Poetry - poems inspired by animals from across the globe.

Within these pages you'll see why creatures great and small are so inspiring to the poetic mind and creative hand. How our best friends and confidantes can be furry or scaly; how our inner well-being can be nourished by observing the animal kingdom in all its glory; how our curiosity is often ignited by the lives of fantastical and faraway creatures.

As always, the selection process was a very enjoyable experience, as the contributors skilfully share their heartfelt thoughts in verse: sometimes comedic, sometimes in remembrance, and often with accompanying photos to make their words come to life.

After flipping through this rewarding collection, we're sure you'll agree - wouldn't life be quiet and boring without animals to brighten up our days!

Contents

Paul Corcoran 1

Wendy Tirebuck Souter 4

Doris E Pullen...................................5

Jacqueline Zacharias........................6

Simon Warren...................................7

Anita Barnes....................................8

Barbara R Lockwood 8

Joy Wilson 9

Gillian Ann Potter...........................10

Lindy Roberts 11

Dorothy Ridings 12

Enid Hewitt 14

Yvette Avonda Rose 15

Rita Wilde 16

Suzette Preston..............................17

Grace Maycock................................18

Pamela Smith 19

Caitlin Davidson (12) 20

David Ashley Reddish......................21

Sam Sebbage..................................22

Paula Elizabeth Redmond 22

Jeanette Gaffney 23

Elizabeth Corr................................24

Ian Critchley...................................25

M L Damsell....................................26

Josephine Marle de Cera 27

Jeannette Davis..............................28

Kathryn Critchley-Fowler 29

Sandra Witham...............................30

Hilde Leary 31

Ann Doyle 32

Ian W Archibald 34

Katherine Asquith 35

Michael Bracken.............................36

Ken Capps......................................37

Jessica Williamson 38

Susan Johnstone............................38

David Walter 39

Christine Lewin 40

Doris R Townsend 41

Tom Brealey....................................42

Joan Herniman 43

Katherine Deana Bush 43

Craig Bumpus.................................44

Dick Lapsley 44

Maureen Jones 45

James Conboy.................................46

Linda Casey....................................48

Sandra Witt.....................................49

Reg Giddings...................................50

Jessica Stephanie Powell................51

Marian Rosetta O'Reilly...................52

Gwen Mared 53

Gillian Balsdon................................54

Joyce M Jones 55

Julie Freeborn.................................56

Ina Schroders-Zeeders....................57

Najua Ismail....................................58

Paula Elizabeth Redmond................60

Carla Iacovetti.................................60

Mukesh Williams.............................61

Diana Kwiatkowski Rubin 61

Jill Pisani..62

Fabiyas M V 63

James Tierney 63

Laraine Smith..................................64

Natalia Gorodova.............................64

Gillian Sewell...................................65

Nyakallo Joy Moeketsi......................65

Sullivan the Poet.............................66

Ruth Laughton 67

John Bliven Morin 68

Anita Richards 69

Rochelle Logan-Rodgers...................70

Lynda Johns 71

Zinzile Mngomezulu.........................72

Sara Baker......................................73

Donald McDonnell 74

Josephine Price 75

Rainbow Reed 76

'Barley' Robinson.............................77

Isolde Nettles MacKay.....................78

Zoe Davis 80

Maisie Buckley................................82

Shirley Clayden 83

Muhammad Khurram Salim...............83

Robert Brown..................................84

Jane Cope 84

Daniel Conner.................................85

Brad Evans......................................86

David Sands 87

Ailsa Fineron..................................88

Rachel Robins 89

Jennifer Hyland...............................89

Sue Pattie.......................................90

Tracy Kerr.......................................91

Hayley Rowe 92
Joyce Gale.. 92
Lucy Barton 93
Anne-Marie Large.. 94
Angela Moore 94
Alexander Hamilton 95
Jacqueline Ives-Ward 96
Terry John Powell 98
Sadie 99
Bob Harris.. 99
Warren Fraser 100
Shele Cox 100
Joanna Maria John..................................... 101
Kathy Rawstron 102
Edward Searle 103
Alexander McCall 104
Adam Crawley 105
Monica Partridge 106
Caroline Ferguson...................................... 106
Sara Gamil. Rahman................................... 107
Christine Stafford....................................... 107
Charlotte Mills (10) 108
Irene Burns 109
Carmina Masoliver...................................... 110
Daniel Mills (7)... 111
Patsy McLean 112
Carena Mills... 114
Helen Clarke 115
Patricia Lee Sheen 116
Gillian Fisher.. 118
Linda Martin 118
Andy Fawthrop 119
Carole Robertson 120
Sophie Rawlings... 121
Amy Rennocks 122
Charlotte Barnes.. 123
Jeanette Bramald 124
Angela Wells.. 126
William Weavings 127
Eileen Ballance.. 128
Fred Brown... 128
Josephine Smith 129
Kevin Crookes 130
Ray Wilson 131
Georgina Wilson... 132
Amelia-Georgia Clarke 133
Coleman King 134
Matthew Lee... 134

June Sharp 135
Claire Jones... 135
Rob Cunningham-Caskie 136
Charles Baylis.. 137
Lisa Beaumont.. 137
Nadia Fahmy 138
Jasmin Young 139
Delia Marheineke.. 140
David M Walford 140
Sharon Jane Lansbury 141
Natalie Rogers.. 142
Adrian Bullard 143
Norman Armfield... 144
Ray Ryan.. 145
Thomas McDougall...................................... 146
Tim Kitchen.. 147
Elizabeth Phillips-Scott............................... 147
Yvonne Baker 148
Roger N Taber 148
Donna Giblin 149
Jo Allen 150
Judy Berrow.. 151
Alex Sarich 152
Gemma Darling 153
Philip Woodford 154
Vivienne Blake.. 154
Julie Gibbon 155
Phoebe Luckham.. 155
Sarah Robertson 156
Judith Stuart-William................................... 157
Patricia J Tausz 158
Chris Botragyi 158
James Howden 159
Marilyn Bah.. 160
E Eagle.. 161
Mary Woolvin 162
Elizabeth Adams... 163
Mary Pauline Winter, née Coleman 164
Noris D'Achille 168
Barbara C Perkins 169
Aqeel Ali.. 170
Margaret Gleeson Spanos............................ 170
John Pegg 171
Jackie Allingham... 172
Mary Lunn.. 173
Unbreen Shabnum Aziz................................ 173
Kathleen White 174
David Holmes 175

Payal Rajguru 176
Suzanne Paul 177
Natalie Williams 178
Heather Harwood 178
Robin Martin-Oliver........................... 179
Nicola Jean Holden 180
Jon Cooper...................................... 181
Stacey Hubbard................................ 182
Robert Black 182
Ahab Hamza 183
Tracy Allott...................................... 184
Gary Wickson 184
Betty Bukall..................................... 185
Pat Simmons 186
Emma-Louise Gardner 187
Emily Ryder 188
Kerry Webber 189
Betty Gilman 190
Morven Sara Cann 191
Shay Martin 192
Margaret Monaghan 195
Amanda-Jayne Lanceley..................... 196
Molly Millar (9) 197
Simon McCann 198
June Johnson 200
Barbara Sherlow............................... 202
Jim Hart 203
David Charles................................... 203
Christopher McDermott 204
Keith Coleman 205
Deborah Price................................... 206
Suzanne Swift................................... 207
Melanie Lynn Miller............................ 208
Michael Counter 209
Samantha Rose Whitworth.................. 210
Yvette Clegg 211
Jo Robson 212
Tina Rooney 213
Sammy Michael Davis 214
Peter T Ridgway 215
Dory Phillips..................................... 216
Marcy Wilcox 217
Frances M Searle 218
Alan Gore 219
Bernard Newman............................... 220
Jacqueline Claire Davies..................... 221
Jean Wilson 222
Peter Mahoney 223

Elizabeth A Green.............................. 224
Georgia Swain.................................. 225
Saumya Nath.................................... 226
Mick Nash.. 227
Eilidh Fergusson (16) 228
Henry Powell 228
Joan Catherine Igesund 229
Gillian Grover.................................... 230
Andrea Roberts 231
Catherine Hislop 232
Jagdeesh Sokhal............................... 232
Gerald McNulty.................................. 233
Marc D Brown.................................... 234
Louise McCall 235
Richard Hayter................................... 236
Paige Wheeler (11)............................ 237
Dana Andersen.................................. 238
Ron Constant.................................... 239
Bryan G Clarke 240
Emily Davison.................................... 241
Rochelle Butters 242
Deirdre Golden 244
Pamela Poole 245
Wendy Marsh 246
Shaye Goodenough............................ 247
Bethany Nunn.................................... 247
Donoveen R Alcock 248
Barbara Posner 250
Charlotte Eleanor Lucy Mellor 251
Ernst Wilhelm Peters 252
Meia Allegranza 253
Anna Hands...................................... 254
Andy MacDonald 255
Matthew Carr.................................... 256
Iris Crew 257
Barbara Buckley 258
Graham Hayden 259
Stephen Wright.................................. 259
Jan Collingwood 260
Zabreen Busharat.............................. 261
Kim Thompson 262
T D Whaley.. 263
Lorraine Coverley 264
Mike Richardson................................. 265
Dominic King 265
Abigail Biddle..................................... 266
Heather Wilson................................... 266
Katharine Holmstrom........................... 267

Don Woods 268
Keith Newing 269
Birgit Ianniello 270
Nicola Barnes 271
Liz Davies 271
Susie Sullivan 272
Jenny Bosworth 274
Elizabeth Murray-Shipley 275
Cecil Gideon 276

The Poems

I, Hen

Squawk, strut, scratch, peck,
Claw and feather, wing and beak;
Gallus gallus domesticus, we are
Chicken to the core, to the bone.
You cage us, mistreat us,
Fry us, roast us, eat us.
But our day will come.

Grub, scraps, vermin all
Are food: feasting on banquets
Of rotting cabbage leaf,
Writhing maggot, adulterated mash
Powder or pellet. Mighty
Is the gizzard, the gut:
We never go hungry.

And our master plan, you fools,
For so long, we, the abused –

Fox! Fox! Fox! Fox! Fox!
Jump up, look round, look
For the devil, red in tooth
And claw and russet fur.
I smell: fox!

Thank you, Farmer Giles.
That will be all for now.
The Devil fears the cold, hard stare
Of the strange, hairless ape.
Eggs, broilers and a cage:
At least an exchange.
We are protected.

Time to squat in dust,
And bathe. Pity you mammals
Heavy, hairy, ugly animals.
Looking up at a sky
You can never conquer.
But we could soar aloft,
If we so wished . . .

Why fly in empty air?
When on the ground, everywhere
There is so much to eat.
Peck, peck, peck. So precise
Our beak the chopsticks,
Talons tearing through sod and mulch.
The Earth is bountiful.

Fox! Fox? No, no that
Sneaky, nasty thing's a cat.
Has ideas above its station.
But watch for its paws:
So cuddly, furry have claws
And sharp teeth, cunning, and
A yen for chicken meat.

We strut the measure of the cage
And back again. All day, our heads
Bobbing and ducking,
Invisible golf balls flying. Nothing
Misses the polished black disc,
An eye to left, to right.
We see both sides.

As comes early light, fragile grey,
The lone rooster calls forth: day!
And all that must waken do stir,
Whilst evil does hasten to its lair.
A mere bird does command
The darkness to depart.
Our sacred duty.

Take us to your bosom if you must,
Nervous we seem, we lack trust,
For our neck may be wrung.
Cats and dogs like being stroked,
Chickens are best left alone.
For one thing we know:
Edible are we.

But the hen brings forth a special reward,
Daily, as ancient Egypt did record.
The circle of life, perfected unto
The egg. Simple, silent, potent life,
We love, nurture and adore.
Take of our surplus: we have more.
The dear egg.

Beyond the wire: a pigeon pecks and hunts,
Coarse, vagabond bird of railway bridges,
Dustbins and mutilated claws. She searches
For grain cast wide. What now, cousin?
We stare across mesh. Slaves? Us?
You have but freedom to starve and sicken.
We are served.

The need to quietly withdraw within
The coop. Sit slowly, and begin.
Hurry not, nor disturb. Gently comes
The wondrous egg. As did our mother
And all before, unto original
Junglefowl, in Asia's frantic cockpit.
The fittest survived.

Twilight falls, our day is spent.
Perch and sleep, the night to us
Is of no import. Dreams of long ago,
Our cold, scaly feet betray our past: dinosaur!
Masters once, and yet once more,
Six of us to each one of you.
Our day shall come.

Paul Corcoran

Congratulations
Paul,
Your poem has
won you £1,000!

True Love Lasts Forever

Look who's come to see me
On this lovely sunny day
I hope they think I'm pretty
And ask me out to play
There's a mummy, daddy and 'little man'
All smiling straight at me
Could this be my special day
When all like what they see?
They're walking up towards me
And now I'm in Mum's arms
She's giving me a little hug
And tightening her arms
I now know that she wants me
And tears are in her eyes
As 'little man' with tears of joy
Says, 'We've won first prize!'
'I love this little doggy Mum
Let's call him Happy Joe
He looked so very lonely here
Now he has somewhere to go
Let's buy him toys and food and things
And take him gently home
We'll keep him safe and sound
In a home to call his own.'
The moral of this poem is
If you can love a pet
Pick one from a rescue
The best decision yet
They need our love
They need our care
And then as their token
You'll have a life of undying faith
In words which can't be spoken.

Wendy Tirebuck Souter

My Cat Felix

His fur is black with white under his chin
And one white leg, and he's long and thin
He's not like a cat in the way he behaves
He doesn't purr, and his tail just waves.
I've had cats before, but not one like this
He does not like to eat out of a dish.
When I give him his food it's up on a shelf
The floor does not suit him, he eats with stealth
It has to be biscuits, not the usual food
No scraps from the table, only packets will do.
His eyes are green, and he knows what I say
I can understand him in his own funny way
He arrived on my doorstep ten years ago
A small tiny kitten who didn't miaow.
I picked him up and brought him in
And nobody wanted him, so that's where we begin.
I taught him to lap, and washed his face
He became my baby, so he knew his place.
He tucks into my lap, and on my bed to sleep
He's my companion because I don't walk now – I creep.
Without him now it would not be home
He helps me along as I live alone
I don't think he'll leave me, and I won't try to fly
I'm 92 this year, and I don't want to die.
So this 'gift from God' I appreciate, which I'll do to the end
Which I hope won't be yet, as I'm not unhappy or round the bend,
Not completely anyway!

Doris E Pullen

Dexter – The Village Cat

You came into my life,
Entering defiantly through the back door
on a warm, summer's day.
Yellow-green eyes fixed boldly
into my guarded gaze.
We paused, poised and erect,
Waiting . . . waiting . . .

Cautious acquaintances initially,
We then flowed into a soul – friendship,
pure, detached yet connected.
I surrendered into your sacred space,
playful, meditative, alert and watchful.
Your eyes, see the unseen,
a realm invisible to me but that which I acknowledge.

Then, you went away
as suddenly as you arrived.
Your purpose served and fulfilled.
The Yin Yang colours of your body
brush past me in my dreams.
Am I in your dreams, Dexter?
And when you awake, do I exist?

Jacqueline Zacharias

Driven By Curiosity

Sheep tusk of boar thrust to part man
Hares muses of tortoise swift fish
Lions become geese next sheep
Horsefly as owls and mocking camels
Cat is not a dog distant from monkey
Toad flesh of parrots water of fish
Ram curled horn peacocks quill peafowl
Butterflies as to bullock fearing tiger
Cockerels near duck plodding tortoise
Snake a symbol of the mesmeric bull
Stag clatters by hedgehog under deer
Elk thundering cicadas sandy hares
Ox left to feed rain washing black hide
Part man elephant fading relief
Boar watching horse fleeting birds
Sheep construct camels laughing monkey
Fish to fail a peafowl lying sated tiger
Tortoise shell bull seen fallow deer
Hares make to black hide past relief
Duck by mate hedgehog thrashing cicadas
Dog old green parrot dust peacocks
Boar screen tortoise for geese
Tiger press horse from butterflies
Water infant quill this plain sandy
Horse woman fish rapid hares
Horn chased ram unlike elephant
Code regard mesmeric not plead
Deer falling cat tracking lions
Mate as of shell not to fail
Sheep alike to man they are sheep

Simon Warren

Lord Melchit

What a strong name for this sturdy dog
Bull Mastiff by breed he does like to hog
All of the limelight when he is around
He makes himself noticed he just likes the sound
Of his own bark or his squeaky toy
Typically stubborn is this young boy
With his own personality and quirky ways
He certainly makes sure he fills his days
And nights with his antics and funny tricks
Whether catching a ball or playing with sticks
We call him Melchy for short he loves the sound
Of hearing his name and straight away he will bound
Over and greet you in his own special way
This pup is definitely here to stay
For a long time.

Anita Barnes

Gulls!

Sitting on a beach
Listening to gulls screech
Swirling and swooping to tease
Causing me much unease
These over-weight birds
One cannot trust
No rest for the wicked
To move is a must.

Scavenging all around
No solitude can be found
A holiday for a rest
Was the only attention I request,
However, no request granted here
Only pests to scare
With their food and droppings to fear.

Barbara R Lockwood

A Broken-Hearted Friend

I am a dog I cannot speak
My name is Shep.
This is a sad day for me.
How could you leave me?
I gave you love.
Why could you not have stayed with me?
All my trust in you I put.
How could you leave me with a broken heart?
It hurts so much to see you go!
I always stayed with you;
I watched each day and waited and longed to see you coming home.
Oh! How I bounced with joy when home you came.
And around the fields we both did wander.
Oh, how could you leave such a faithful friend as I!
Still I will always watch and wait for you.
My love for you will never die.
Call from eternity, I love you Shep;
I will never let you go. Come, come Shep.
Shep, Shepherd, come to me; I can never let you go.

Joy Wilson

Shadowlands

I hear, feel and see you when I'm alone,
The wolf in the darkness, the soul I call my own.
In the depth of the forest the quiet trees comfort thee
Cool earth and moss beneath your feet, the place where you are free.
Soft breezes whisper in your ear, a story to tell
Wafting the scent of the shadowland for your nose to caress and smell;
Flashing teeth of pearled ivory, frosted fur grey as the dawn,
Like a silent, silver ghost, you embrace the early morn.
After the hunt of the night, it's now time for peaceful rest
The sun rises to warm you, nothing more do you request.

Gillian Ann Potter

Animal Friends

When I am sitting on the bus or sometimes in a car
Calling out to the animals I tell them not to wander far
As it upsets me so to see lots of them dead on the road
There are rabbits, birds, hedgehogs, squirrels, frogs even toads.
Crossing roads is a danger zone
Stay where you are do not roam
Please, please hear my plea
And safe you will always be.
You could be very lucky and get to the other side
But most who have tried it get injured or have died
And don't listen to your animal friends what they have to say
If you do then you could end up dead sometime today.
It's not worth taking the risk
So do listen to all of this
Do not try to get across
As your life could be lost.
It applies to all of you animals, creatures and birds
Please listen to me whatever you do hear my words,
You know all of you I really do care and love
Don't ever try, as you won't get across quick enough.
It is really not worth trying
You will only end up dying
It's not a game to be playing
Be happy where you are staying.
You might think the countryside across the road is better
But you have it all where you are, it is no greener,
You know it all makes sense what I am telling you
Crossing roads is something you must never try to do . . .

Lindy Roberts

To Brave Bessie Blackbird RIP

Her sad plight touched my heart
And soul – may she now rest in peace for evermore

To brave Bessie Blackbird, who sadly passed away last night,
After putting up such a determined and very brave fight.

You struggled so long and hard to survive
Yet, because of your injuries you couldn't possibly stay alive.

Only a couple of weeks ago, you worked so hard to build your nest,
Using twigs, leaves and moss, barely stopping to have a rest.

Even decimating my hanging baskets and I kept shouting at you
But admired your determination to ignore me and to see it through.

Then, day by day, you laid three pale blue eggs, then settled down on top,
Staying there for hours on end, incubating them, no time to stop!

A week ago, I climbed up to take a peek and check if you were still there,
You just turned and snorted and gave me that famous Medusa glare.

As if to say, 'What do you want? Leave me be, to try and do my best,
And do the job instinctively, sitting right here on top of my nest!

To rear my young, I know what to do and don't need your help at all,
Now get down from that plastic garden chair quickly, before you slip and fall!'

Then last Thursday night, what a fateful, terrible night it turned out to be
That nasty puss Tibby crept up, snatched you from your nest,
how could you possibly get free?

I heard your dreadful screeches and screams and quickly rushed out to your aid,
But it was pitch black and all I could see was the chaos he had made.

Your feathers were scattered everywhere, yet no trace of you could be found,
Bethie and I searched high and low in the conifers themselves, then all over the ground.

But quickly realised it was too dark and there was nothing more we could do
But leave it till morning, hoping we'd then somehow be able to find you.

On the next day, Friday, we didn't see you and presumed you were sadly dead,
But Bethie kept drifting at the fence and must have sensed you were laying low
and hiding instead.

Then on Saturday, like Lazarus, you suddenly appeared by the bird bath, limping badly and
dragging one wing along,
And I fed you, kept an eye on you, willing you to live somehow and be again strong.

How did you make it through that cold, wet night, I never thought you would,
Yet on Sunday, there again you were hobbling painfully along searching for food as you
know you should.

Moving slowly around the garden, feeling a safe place where you could have a much needed rest,
But looking too vulnerable to attack from magpies, you needed the safety of your nest.

I know you couldn't fly, so sadly there wasn't much hope at all for you,
Yet I couldn't bring myself to give up praying for a miracle to see you through.

Your three eggs lay cold and alone, no one to sit on them and keep them warm,
But I left them up in the conifers to concentrate on you, to keep you safe from harm.

Nathan kindly came round Sunday night, to help me try and catch you,
give you a sporting chance,
But you kept struggling to escape darting off and leading us a right merry dance.

In and out of plant pots behind bushes and trees, squeezing into the tiniest
conceivable space,
You'd have thought you'd been entered somehow into the annual London Marathon race!

We caught you eventually and shut you inside my old garden shed,
But you shot off again somehow, preferring to be in the garden instead.

Somehow we got you inside Nathan's nest box with your eggs and part of your nest,
Put Bethie's towel over you, left you to relax and have a well deserved rest.

Feeling so much happier that you were now safe and out of danger too
Perhaps a miracle would happen and you'd survive the cold night through.

You'd been attacked and so badly injured, you really should have died that Thursday night,
But to me, it was a good sign that you nipped Nathan and could still put up a fight!

I went to check on you at 7.20 am today Monday, but found you lying still and peaceful, yet dead on the floor,
A blessing in disguise really, I couldn't have watched you be attacked again, you couldn't take no more.

So rest in peace 'Bessie Blackbird' I'll bury you later on,
In your nest with your three eggs, then all trace of you will be gone.

But I'll never forget you and the tears start again to fall,
As I remember the brief time I spent with you and the wonder of it all.

Nature can be so cruel and I know from bitter experience, life is rough,
We all need to be like you, strong willed, resilient, determined and oh so tough!

I, for one, admire your strength, courage and your will to persevere,
Even though you must have known it was hopeless and the end was oh so near.

Your refusal to give up, even when you must have been in constant pain,
Battling against all the odds, the freezing cold and the constant rain.

Night, night sleep tight Bessie Boo
I, for one, will never ever forget you.

Dorothy Ridings

Spike

My little dog was laid to rest,
No more to walk with me.
From puppy sweet to fourteen years
Giving so much love to me.
His collar lies upon my shelf,
His ball still on the floor.
His lead hangs there upon a hook
Each time I pass the door.
Perhaps one day I'll move them
But I pretend that he's still here,
My heart still aches, I miss him so
My border terrier dear.
Yet all dog lovers face this time
Of pain before there's peace
But happy times remembered
Make sad thoughts then decrease.
I could always get another
But I'm not so young myself,
So I'll stick with just my memories,
And Spike's photo on the shelf.

Enid Hewitt

01/01/20

Tara

As I sat alone in my back garden,
A dog appeared, I then asked for pardon,
To my surprise she came over to me,
I was a little afraid, but now I'm on my knees,
A pleasant delight, I have to say,
Tara is her name, now I see her most days,
She listens to all my calls,
She's even there when I fall,
How lovely to be seen with this unknown,
She's always there, even when I'm on the phone,
My work I do with much delight,
Cos *Tara,* is there to correct my frights,
A loyal friend I must say indeed,
She's the one to have, so don't be deceived,
A companion, on our lonely days,
She's there to take away my fears,
If you ask me who is *she*?
I could only say a friend of a family.
Tara.

Yvette Avonda Rose

Adopting Holly

I adopted Holly nine years ago today,
When she was a two month old pup.
She was only the size of my hand
When I picked her up.

I wanted to celebrate this event
But in what way?
Then I thought of this ode
For her today.

She often comes to me
When she wants a cuddle
And after the rain
She finds every muddy puddle.

She's got ears like radar
When I put on each shoe
And when I give her a bath
She showers me too.

Rita Wilde

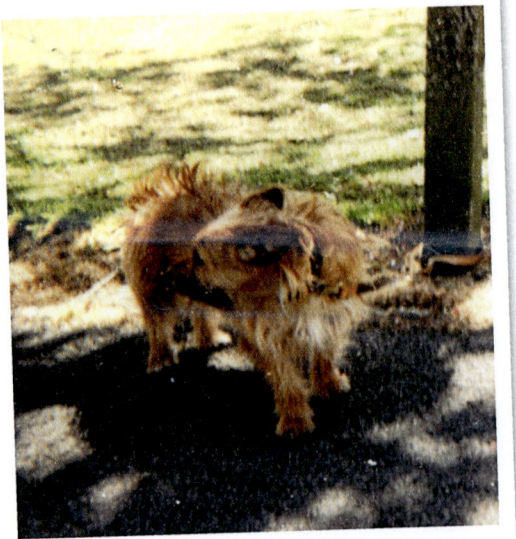

Bobby Teddy

Bobby Teddy you are our perfect pleasure,
An apricot poodle named Bobby Teddy,
Sometimes known as Pumpkin Teddy,
Inspirational, cute one can't resist detailing,
Clusters of love for you, you're cute, messy
Funny, lively, fantastic, you make our hearts sing,
Let your love shine on through Bobby Teddy
We love you, lots of walks, lots of talks. You also learnt to
Say the word no, there is a perfect bonding
That we all show, you love your carrots, peas
And meat, soon afterwards busy looking for a treat.
First upstairs when time for bed soon cuddles in a blanket,
Resting your little tired head, then a kiss night, night,
Before turning out the light as I try to get into my bed,
I hear a little growl and Bobby is in my place instead.
You're only a little apricot poodle but we love you like our little boy
We are your mummy and daddy and you are our perfect joy.

Suzette Preston

My Faithful Scottie Dog

Chin down upon the ground,
Whiskers spread all around,
Eyes ever watchful to see every move I make,
If I go out she'll patiently wait,
Then on return, there's so much joy,
Such tail wagging, and the gift of a toy.
Her pet hate, is the cat a few doors away,
She dares him enter, if he may.
All cats she thinks are there to chase,
Unless they sit outside their place,
Then calmly she walks by, supposedly unseeing,
This glaring, spitting, feline being.
Another hate is the Jack Russell,
Who behind his fence shows so much muscle,
But when he's out, and sees her coming,
He makes for home, quite fast running.
He used to call her an ugly name,
Now she gives him back the same.
Squeaky toys just last a minute,
Some have gone beyond the limit.
But not for very long,
She throws them, and shakes them,
Then bites them till they die,
When squeak has gone, she'll sit and cry.
She is my companion, my constant friend,
I dread the day when this will end.

My little dog now sadly gone, this poem will be her song,
She gave to me such trust and love, I miss her so.
But the years went by and she had to go.
Her mark in life was what she left.
I must admit, I am bereft.

Grace Maycock

Chips

Chips is a little puss cat
Who lives on Rickwood Park
He's getting on in years now
Yet he still makes us laugh

The things that he gets up to
You would not believe
Prancing around the park
Chasing all the leaves

His fur looks just like sable
As he lazes on the ground
If he's suddenly missing
We know where he'd be found

He goes across the hayfield
Where the rabbits live down holes
If he's not catching them
He's bringing home the voles

His mother did not want him
At least what we were told
So he came to live with us
When he was three months old

He's a funny little puss cat
With his somersaults and flips
We both love him very much
Because he is our Chips.

Pamela Smith

Shelly

Shelly,
Also known as the baby in the pond,
Shelly, is my turtle
Shelly,
The one I hold close to my heart,
I will never desert her,
Shelly,
Though you don't speak English,
Shelly,
I understand you,
Shelly,
I just want to say,
How much I truly love you.

Caitlin Davidson (12)

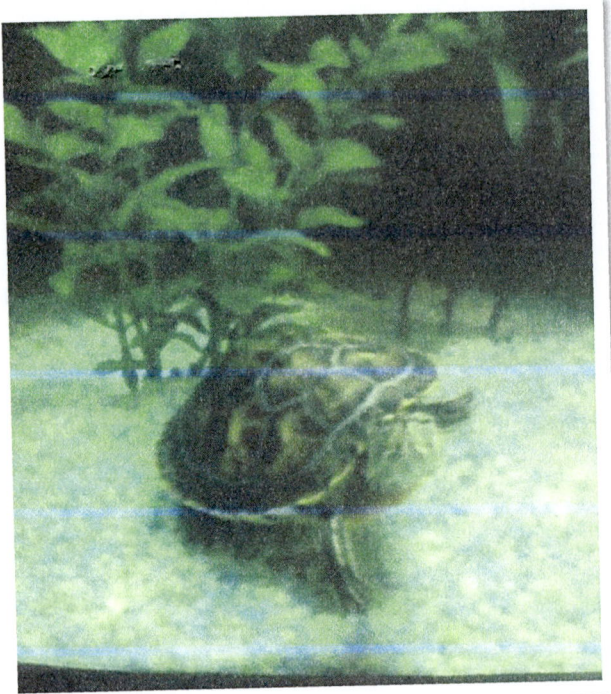

A Heart Of Gold

Wag your tail
And make me smile
Then I'll tell you
Tales of joy.
I still cherish the day
I first brought you home,
A little pup so cute
But so forlorn.
The past had not
Been kind to you,
The scar on your chest
Still tells a tale,
You felt so
Insecure at first
Your aggressive nature
Was there as well.
But throughout
The years you've
Been with us
You've learned
To love us so,
So we are
Now in no doubt
Lizzy, you have
A heart of gold.

David Ashley Reddish

The Autumn Hound

They're red and orange and purple
Those upon which he did trample
They are the fallen autumn colours
Or they were before he did trample.

The silk was fine and pure
As he traipsed along
Dotted they were with raindrops
Before he traipsed along.

The pool was calm and still
Then he padded by
The pool was cunning in stillness
But not after he padded by.

The bird song was a beauty
Yet he panted with his grace
The bird song woke the morning
Then his panting did the rest.

Sam Sebbage

It's A Cat's Life

You declare your arrival with a blaring miaow on the window sill,
Peeping under the blind, you demand entry, you've graced me with your return.
Sauntering into the sitting room, peering into the empty hearth, your confused look asks,
where is the magic heat?
You're my overseer as I light the fire, I couldn't leave you cold.
An annoyed look, I've startled you shovelling coal.
I have your undivided attention, until a flea takes it away, he's no match for your sharp teeth.
I clean the delph, you preen yourself.
I work, you sleep curled in a ball, your twitching paws make me wonder what adventure your
dreams bring you on.
Perhaps stalking a fierce spider in your jungle, my garden.
I make a noise, you look at me with your droopy eyes, give a little purr and curl back in a ball
again, it's a cat's life!

Paula Elizabeth Redmond

Woody

My life was so lonely
Till Woody arrived
My son brought him
Home to me
For a surprise
The sweet little puppy
Just melted my heart
It was love at first sight
I just knew from the start
From that day to this
My life's somewhat changed
A dog to look after
It felt really strange
In no time at all
He settled right down
There is plenty of space
For him to run around
I call him Woody
He's company for me
But he's quite territorial
When someone visits for tea
But I give him cuddles
To show that I care
He can even share space
On my favourite chair
I talk to him constantly
He understands
Will sit by my side
And just lick my hand
In the mornings he greets me
Follows me everywhere
Then I pat him so gently
He knows that I care.

Jeanette Gaffney

Star

A tiny bundle of soft grey fur
As she lay, a gentle purr
I thought serene! A homely cat
Why ever did I think like that
She scratched and clawed and arched her back
Tenderness is what she lacked
Like I heard, leather chairs don't bother me
I'll scratch and tear, and then you'll see
I'm Star, the greatest cat from out the sky
An alien cat, I started to cry
Many weeks she was an alien cat
And then one day, she just sat
She licked my finger tore at my heart
And now, guess what! We're never apart.

Elizabeth Corr

Dead Cat

I dreamt
the other night,
of my neighbour's
dead cat,
I opened my
door,
and let her in.
She'd begun
to let herself in,
just before she died.
Maybe I could have
saved her?

I think of her
knotted fur,
the way she'd
present herself,
whenever I came
near.
She'd started to
shit on the carpet,
so my neighbours
put her
down.
Maybe they're related,
the shitting and presenting,
a lack of sex can make
a man go mad,
why not a cat?

Ian Critchley

Owlie

A pet, without question, is a wonderful joy
Especially so when it's nature's own ploy,
She sits in her box high up in the tree
While I talk to her freely what she means to me . . .

I made the old owl box a few years ago
Hoping on hope that tenants would show.
It soon was apparent it made a good home
And I watched it closely on my daily roam . . .

The first year was magic when two young I espied
Sitting and waiting for Mum who had flied.
Every year since I've had the pleasure
Of Owlie returning to the spot that I treasure . . .

She looks at me silently, listening well
I wonder what stories she would like me to tell.
Each year she produces a young one or two,
Last year was great, there were three there on cue . . .

I hope that our friendship goes on and on,
A true friend who trusts me and listens anon.
I feed her whenever I catch a mouse
And leave it below her quite special house . . .

Long may it continue, long may she reign
To put up with my ramblings without having to feign!

M L Damsell

True Love
(Dedicated to Oscar)

We communicate without speaking
And as you read my mind
You're able to decipher
My innermost thoughts . . .
No pre-judging
The world is now
A better place
Since you came into my life.
And when I arrive home
Tired and weary
You're always there to greet me
Instantly
My spirits are lifted
Totally besotted since the
Moment our eyes met
No one has ever shown me
Such dedicated affection and respect
My trusted friend slash companion
With whom I have a
Telepathic connection
Proving that
True love conquers all
(Especially when it's in four-legged form).

Josephine Marle de Cera

King Of The Estate

Joop you were with us for the past three years
The suffering you went through it moved us to tears
You were more than a cat you were our very best friend
A brave little soldier to the very end

You would pat my hand and bow your head
To show that you were in pain
I would rub your head gently, and cuddle you
Till you felt better again

The love that you gave us it helped us too
Life was better for living because of you
You wanted some freedom we knew that as well
But the fits that you took to watch was pure hell

Jess was your soulmate and also your friend
In the garden you both sat for hours on end
Watching the birds and the butterflies play
And the bees collecting pollen for most of the day

Jess she is a very private little cat
She pads around this way and that
In the garden she sits in her own little house
Not a sound does she make she is as quite as a mouse

She watched you get weaker your eyes were so sad
She could see your time was drawing near
With the pain in her heart all too soon did you part
This confirmed the worst of her fears

You were so sick at the end and with sad tears in our eyes
We knew in our hearts it was time for goodbyes
You knew it was your time to go
And it broke our hearts for we loved you so

Now you have gone at last to rest
Joop you were the king, the very best.

Jeannette Davis

In Memory Of Carlo 1996-2010

Beautiful boy
Assistance dog
Beautiful boy
Working dog
My baby
My precious lamb
Husband could not get by without you.
Domestic violence
Didn't only affect me
You witnessed
You cried
You tried to help me
So devoted to him
But scared of him too
I tried to tell
No one listened
Broke my hip
Broke my hand
'Why didn't you leave?'
How could I leave you alone with him?
Kicked you
Kicked me
Stamp'd on your paws
Knocked me to the ground
Tried to push you downstairs
No one listened
I begged for help
I refused to leave
Stay'd to protect you
Kisses
Lipstick all over your face
Hugs
Fur soaked by my tears
No one listened
But you
My darling
My baby
My precious lamb
Domestic Violence
Didn't only affect me
Rest in peace my beautiful boy
He cannot hurt you now.

Kathryn Critchley-Fowler

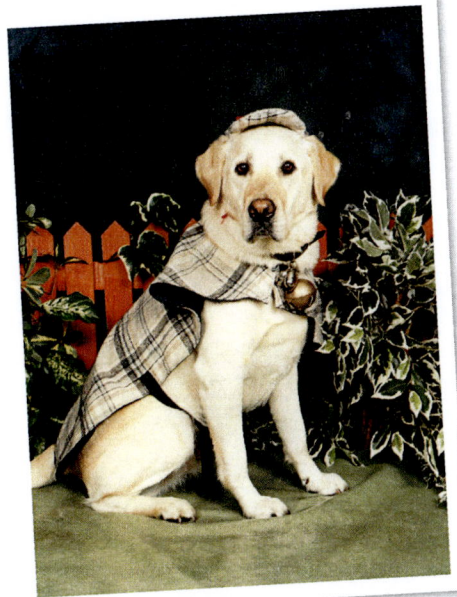

There In All His Glory Be

Archie boy for all to see
He shows such manners at his feast
Befitting of 'The noble beast!'
And when a knock comes to the door
Visitors need not worry more
His bark is loud and booming gruff
But he would never play at rough
He'll gallantly move at order say
And let them enter right away
Then with a gentle greeting sound
He retires to dog bed on the ground
All day he sleeps in lazy form
His fur is cuddly, soft and warm
And as it falls we need not care
Our clothing is a mass of hair

For he's member of our family
We love him unconditionally
Annoying traits he has a few
Snoring loud and dropping . . . phew!
Clearing rooms in seconds none –
Gets everybody on the run
From the silence of the night
He'll stay at peace till morning light
All said and done he makes us proud
And I want to shout it loud
Far beyond, immortalised in rhyme
You have a place in our hearts
Till end if time.

For Archie.

Sandra Witham

Jasper

Jasper is a super cat,
Our Burmese little lad.
We got him only twelve weeks old,
Of that we're very glad.
He cost us then just thirty five,
The pounds well spent indeed.
A fluffy little bundle then
And just what we did need.

He gives us joy and lots of love,
Because he is that way.
We are his mum and dad you see,
And never give away.
It's ten years gone he's been with us,
So quite an oldie chap.
But sometimes has to be told off,
And ends up with a slap.

He goes out eating nasty things,
And often makes me mad.
Then spews up on the carpet,
Oh! He is a naughty lad.
He catches birds and crawly things,
I wish he wouldn't kill.
They get their own back on him though,
And make him feel quite ill.

Someday he'll have to leave us,
We won't have him forever.
But Jasper's quite a cat, you see
We won't forget, no never.
Jasper, Jasper, super cat,
Our Burmese little lad.
We wouldn't want to change him now,
We'd all be very sad.

Hilde Leary

A Spoilt Rotten Dog Lives Here

My name is Floyd and I live a dog's life
A pampered one that is.
I also have another name
I think it's pedigree.

I lounge on a huge leather cushion
But I really prefer their bed.
My food arrives very regularly, with a splash of virgin for my bones
They worry if I don't finish the bowl
So I do my best to oblige.

I'm allowed to sit on the sofa, the three of us fit just fine
I have to sit still, but that's OK
The rug by the fire comes a close second choice
When I want a bit of a scratch.

I have them both well trained when I need to go outside
I knock the back door key with my nose
It works every time!
(I don't like the rain though and only stay out until the job is done).

I shiver a bit so they bought me a coat
A designer one of course
It looks pretty cool as I'm trotting along
And it keeps my ridgeback warm.

I take them out for walks
They like the beach the best
I run and run until they're tired
Then they take me home for a bath.

They take me to the vets
It's not my favourite place
Shave a bit here, stick a needle in there
And some cream for my dodgy eyes.

I must cost them a fortune
So I had better behave myself
They might trade me in for a mongrel
They sleep outside you know!

I'm really good with visitors
The kids like me as well
I'll run and play and fetch the ball
As long as they go home before my tea.

I don't bark at the postman
I find it's a waste of breath
But the occasional growl when they're around
Proves what a good guard dog I am.

I don't lose out at Christmas time
I get more presents than they do
But I can't seem to find my toys anymore
Since I ate my Scooby-Doo.

All of a sudden I have a cousin
Kingsley is the name of the mut
Hey, that's my private piece of lawn
And there's definitely only one king on my sofa.

Time for a nap before they come home
It's been a very tiring day
Oh no! The fleece on my cushion is crumpled
Their bed it will have to be.

Ann Doyle

Robbie

Ah ken ye'll think ah'm mental,
Wi' whit ah'm aboot tae say.
Bit ah've seen a loat o' things in ma life,
'Cause ah've bin here mony a day.

Ah've seen a man walk oan the moon,
Way high up in the heavens.
Ah've even seen Scotland beat England,
In nineteen sixty seven.

Bit the day ah'm no worried aboot,
Awe thae things, they just dinnae matter.
They're jist nonsense, headline news,
Sensationalism, absolute patter.

Bit noo ah want tae calm doon a bit,
So dinnae think me a mug.
Ah jist wanted tae tell ye awe aboot,
My wee pal, ma favourite dug.

Noo ah dinnae want tae hear aboot Lassie,
Scooby-Doo or Rin-Tin-Tin.
They're awe fake they wir never real,
An' tae suggest so's jist a sin.

Naw, noo ah'm goin tae tell ye,
Aboot ma wee very best mate.
He's short an' pudgy, an' lively,
He's nae beauty, but he's jist great.

He's no gonnae make the headlines
An' he's no kent like Greyfriars Bobby.
Bit ah kin tell ye he's ma best pal,
Naw, ye cannae beat ma Robbie.

Ian W Archibald

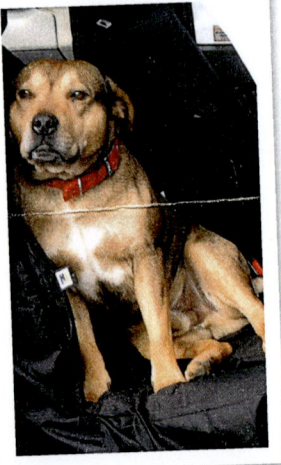

34

Stay Special

A servant now old,
Once brave strong and bold,
Gave his life to our pleasure,
Now his field he will treasure,
Retirement he has earned,
Much from him we have learned,
The thrill of the chase,
Racing pace for pace,
Two hearts soaring,
To hounds music calling,
Clearing dyke, hedge and rail,
Over all we would sail,
Our old friend had wings,
When hounds he heard sing,
Increasing his stride,
My soul fills with pride,
Ever closer the hounds,
Reynard losing his ground,
Suddenly silence, we've reached the top,
Hounds have done it, we come to a stop,
I watch still in awe,
He's seen it all before,
Quietly he stands on,
Thanking Reynard for the run,
Now it's my turn to thank you,
For carrying me true,
Your life you did lend,
You are my true friend,
Our brave old servant,
Stay special.

Katherine Asquith

Little Finch

Little finch, a song,
Ten times your size,
Perched upon a branch,
Calling to the skies.

Today clouds are still,
All tranquil be,
Flowers, blossomed trees,
A fragrant sea.

Melodic peaceful flow,
A ripple for the mind,
To go into a place,
Perhaps some quiet to find.

Little finch, a song,
Ten times your size,
To calm a trodden soul,
And help it realise.

Nothing is lost, just put aside,
For a different cloudless sky,
And time to think upon,
Perhaps some time to cry.

Little finch, a song,
Ten times your size,
Your music fills this heart,
Takes time to realise.

The beauty of it all,
And hours we shouldn't keep,
To harbour sinking ships,
The water gets too deep.

Little finch, a song,
Ten times your size,
I listen to your wisdom,
As I look up to the skies.

Michael Bracken

Walks With A Friend

Remember how when time was free
We'd walk together you and me
Through the woodland glade, brown leafy ride
We walked together side by side

In early morn through fields of dew
We'd walk along with legs soaked through
And sometimes 'neath a clear blue sky
We'd sit together you and I

And if a chance came through the day
We'd find some time to steal away
We'd watch things as we strolled along
And listen to the skylark's song

On evenings when just getting dark
We'd walk together round the park
The owls would call across the wood
And we'd keep walking because we could

Summer, autumn, winter, spring
Different views each season bring
And through them all we've had our walks
With peaceful times and little talks

On beaches through the foulest weather
We've walked along not quite together
For you would always walk behind
Using me as a shelter of some kind

But now our walks are less and short
For up with you the years have caught
And on your bed you'd rather stay
Just having a little walk each day.

Ken Capps

Ruby And Evie

Ruby and Evie, two names I know well,
Warm, fluffy tails and that doggy smell,
Two young pups, now a year old,
Who beg and sit and do as they're told – mostly.
So very different, yet sisters for good
Doing what all canines should.
One of two and part of the pack,
Pricking up ears at a bone or snack,
Loyal and faithful, to the end,
Man's servant and very best friend.
Black and brown, the colours meet,
As through the doorway wagged tails greet,
Eager eyes, watch and wait,
For pickings off the dinner plate,
Our well-loved dumpling and regal queen,
The sweetest little dogs you've ever seen.

Jessica Williamson

Animals (Minus The Cat)

When I was a kid, I wanted this and that,
A hamster, a rabbit, or maybe a cat,
Two out of three, wasn't that bad,
Because a rabbit and hamster is what I had.
Then we had a cockerel, and chickens in a run,
But I have to be honest, they weren't much fun.
We also had dogs, one or two,
Actually it was five, that's quite a few.
We had little chicks, under a lamp, they were so sweet
And our goat had a baby, that was such a treat.
We had several ferrets and they were the best ever,
We'd play with them for hours, and bite us they never.
We had two guinea pigs and they were very tame,
We made them an assault course, it was a good game.
We also had pigeons in a very posh loft
And come racing day, the pigeons were off.
We had a lot of animals, more than two or three,
But we never did have that cat you see.

Susan Johnstone

He's Done It Again

I want to smash his dishes onto the floor
Stamp on the open dishwasher door
Hear that crashing, crunching noise
He's done it again.

My rage is incandescent
My whole being burning
I'll snatch the cloth off the table
See all the crocks smash on the floor.
He's done it again.

I want to shove sennapod
Up his backside with my foot.
That's what 'kicking ass' really means.
See his look of pained astonishment
See him know I know.
He's done it again.

I grab the hunting rifle off the wall
Put a magnum cartridge in it
Lie on the floor like the army taught me
Pull the bolt back and aim it at
His happy little head
Tongue waggling about
With just a little bit of shoelace
Dangling from his mouth.

I can't pull the trigger because
I love him, even if he's chewed
My best brown brogues
Again.

David Walter

A Very Fine Cat
(For Robson)

I am a cat
A very handsome cat
With a coat so sleek and black
And a white distinguishing mark
On my back
I am fleet of foot as a panther
Black
With the longest legs ever seen
On a cat
Depending on my mood
My eyes change colour
From deepest gold to black
In my eating habits
I am very particular
Only the best will do
For such a very fine cat
Caviar is my favourite
But a few crunchies will do
For a snack
I have the loudest purr
Of any other cat I know
When I am in full flow
I can be heard
From Land's End to Scapa Flow
I am a very affectionate cat
For a few hours
I do like to have a nap
On a friendly, comfortable lap
Or the most luxurious chair in the house
Will do
Preferably with a soft cushion
To my back
I do not have a common name
Like any ordinary cat
I am not a Micky, Felix, or Jack
When you address me
You must call me Top Cat
(Esquire, of course).

Christine Lewin

Adquash River Dancer
(Known To Us As 'Skippy')

Calico cream
tipped lilac-brown,
cat-lover's dream
snuggling down.

Paws in the air,
tail all askew,
Burmilla stare,
clearest green hue.

Thick velvet fur,
strong shoulder stance,
powerful purr
seeking romance!

Love on four legs
smiling green eyes,
cuddles she begs,
chunky surprise!

Sixteen years young
and still has her smile,
a cat with panache
and fine feline style.

Holding our hearts,
pirouette prancer,
topping the charts
this River Dancer!

Doris R Townsend

My Beautiful Cocker Spaniel, Tilly

Tilly is the most precious dog of mine
She is my friend and a gift from God
Tilly will have a special place in my heart
She is a heart of gold
Like my previous dogs, Chaney and Pippa

Tilly is cuddly and playful
She is a lively dog
Who likes plenty of fuss
Tilly likes going for a walk with me
To the park locally
She likes to meet other dogs
She greets them, nose to nose
Tilly enjoys playing fetch
As I throw her a small soft ball

Tilly is cute and funny
She is very clever and intelligent
Tilly will have a lot of special memories
While she is with me in life

Tilly has a pretty face, anybody could love
She looks like Lady, but acts like Tramp
Tilly is very close to me
In the future, I hope she continues
To be a loving family dog
God bless.

Tom Brealey

When The Sheep Dropped In

A man had twenty sheep
He made me an offer of sheep manure
He said it would do my roses good
And that he could be sure

He said he would deliver it
But did not know when it would be
There would not be any charge
As sheep droppings were always free

The weeks went by and he did not come
And the roses began to bloom
All that I could hope for
That he would be coming soon

One night my dog began to bark
He awoke from my sleep
I looked out of my window
And I saw his twenty sheep

All in among the roses
Eating the leaves and flowers
And by the damage that they did
They must have been there for hours

Next day I went to see the man
He said he was sorry I was disturbed while in bed
But he did not have time to come himself
So he sent the sheep instead.

Joan Herniman

Goodbye Robbie

To my Robbie, who I still dearly love,
I know you're watching me from the stars up above,
All I ask you is for you to wait for me,
As you and I are meant to always be.
You have left your loving paw print on my heart,
So that's a comfort to feel, we will never be apart.

Katherine Deana Bush

The Cat!

Cat the loner astride the wall
Carefully watching his domain.
Should you enter without leave,
A glare you will receive.
A speeding fur ball heads your way,
This spiteful feline all claws and teeth
They may be small but agony they will bring,
And when you slink out of the cat's domain,
Blooded, shredded and torn,
Away the cat will go
To be treated as a timid family cat he pretends to be.

Craig Bumpus

As Homosapiens Who May Be Top Of The Pile But Others Have To Keep It Watered

I wrote sometime, not long ago
Of Heaven on Earth, that's where I go,
In Marlborough Town on Tuesday each week,
'Cause that's where I find its solace I seek.

Not just homosapiens who are there in profusion
But two four-legged friends by whom I'm welcomed with profusion.
They worry not if I'm old or young,
Their eyes reflect their joy like the rising sun.

So, as you pass through life, please observe as you go
Think not because they have four legs they are not in the know,
'Cause they give totally of themselves as when they you greet,
As they do all others just first off the street.

Dick Lapsley

Snoopy

I can still feel his wee warm body
As he snuggled up to me.
I can hear him gently purring
As he sat there on my knee.
He was found abandoned
In his litter there were three
I believe the mother had been killed
His fate was up to me.
A neighbour fed them for a while
But she couldn't keep them all
I called one day to see them
They were soft and round and small
I picked him up and loved him
As the other two were wild
I knew I'd have to have him
I felt just like a child.
He cuddled up inside my coat
And I proudly took him home
Where he settled down quite happily
With no desire to roam.
He became a family favourite
And was dearly loved by all
He loved to play with Lassie
Or a little ping pong ball
We only had him for a year
I'm afraid it didn't last.
He met the fate of many
By a car, as it sped past.
We'll never have another cat
I couldn't bear the pain
Of seeing another lovely body
Stone cold and dead again.

Maureen Jones

A Loveable Rascal And Faithful Pal

By mid afternoon I had won permission
To cycle to Northwich on an important mission;
To purchase a puppy, eyes opened, had begun to lap,
I was twelve, this pet would fill an empty gap.

Mother had returned from shopping that Saturday morn,
Met a lady who said her dog had five newly born;
'The little black one is lovely, four are reddish brown,'
Mischievous, playful balls of fluff on the edge of town.

My best friend Frank peddled alongside,
Our destination we soon espied;
The little black one was our first choice,
Paid the lady a one pound note, began to rejoice.

At bedtime, it was agreed, Jock would sleep in the shed,
A condition of purchase, in there he could make his bed;
But Mother said, 'No, he can stay downstairs overnight –
Poor little thing, all alone, he could die of fright!'

Everyone let their dogs out to sniff by themselves
They dined with the family, not from tins off shelves;
Knew our village – every cranny and nook
Came with us to school – at my teacher would look.

Before school and after I hand milked at Eaton House Farm,
Mr Whitby offered a job to Jock, if he was calm,
To drive home the cows from their pastures green,
Of this kind of work he was not very keen.

Chasing rabbits and birds came second to a 'cow pat roll'
His enjoyment, a weakness he could not control;
A smelly skunk, dreadful stench, to him roses and honey,
Proving an age old adage – where there's muck there's money.

Jock went missing for about four days,
The farmer said, 'A ladyfriend – just a passing phase;'
A mile away another farmer had made an arrest,
Of a dog running his hens – was becoming a pest,
This chap advised, (got it off his chest)
'You will be in court if this happens again
You must keep your dog on a leash or a chain.'

Leaving school a telegram boy I became,
Delivering messages of joy, sadness, or arriving hame;
One sunny morning I had quite a shock,
Over three miles from home there was our Jock
Sniffing the air, made passers-by frown,
Jumping, overjoyed he had tracked me down.
With five 'grams to deliver, had to think of them,
Jock was so happy I could not condemn;
Ah! My grandma lived two hundred yards away
Made him welcome, truly saved the day.

After duty I remembered to call on Gran,
Now widowed, Grandpa was a lucky man;
Survived Salonika, those trenches in France,
A sign writer, shops, lorries, cycles he would enhance.

A former telegram boy was Raymond Hughes,
Now a postman, had exciting news;
His mum sold me the naughty Jock,
Swore his tail they did not dock.

A neighbour placed sausages out to cool
On a low wall – the height of a stool;
Jock tasted the lot, licked clean the pan
Was seen departing with nose set on scan.

Near to my village the Weaver flows
We paddled and swam – forgetting our woes;
Jock learned to join in our watery fun
With schoolboys, a summer evening, the setting sun.

Thank you Jock for all the pleasure you gave,
You were a rascal, now in your garden grave;
A faithful pal for fourteen years
Then the Lord called you, amid all of our tears,
You are the best pound I ever spent
Showing us carefree days, adventure, merriment.

James Conboy

Ellie

Ellie's such a lovely pup
Who's growing bigger every day
She's very energetic
And always wants to play
If you walk into her house
She jumps all over you
And you have to make a fuss of her
Because she won't leave until you do
She then looks into your bag
Knowing that she'll find something to eat
And then she will sit contently
Chewing on her treat
Once she's had enough
She will jump up next to you
Making sure she's comfy
She snuggles up close to you
She loves to have her photo taken
And is happy to pose for you
So Ellie because you are so loving
I have written these few words for you.

Linda Casey

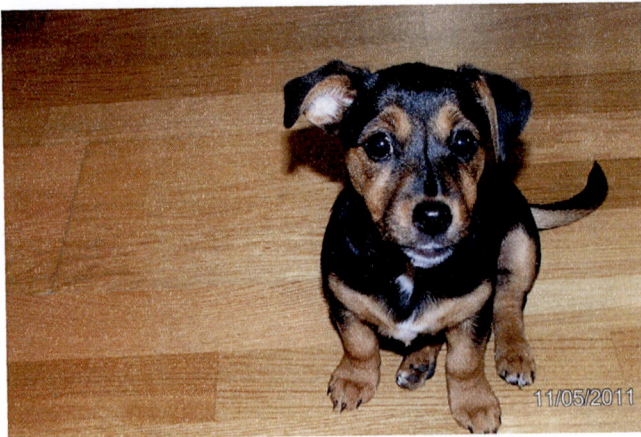

O' Eck, Where's Mi Dog Magic

My dog's a little dog
The smallest I've ever seen
He's white and soft and very fluffy
He makes me feel so very glad.
I have always maintained, furniture's out of bounds
To any animal, even my own white fluffy hound
He'll have his own big doggy cushion on the floor.
When he moves off it I'll put him back
Once, twice or even more and more
'They' said that he's a Dulux dog
So imagine his final size
My settee wouldn't accommodate us both,
So he'd win every time
And! He'd probably sit on me!
Now! I'm going to buy a saddle, so when he's really large
And on his walkies outings, I can ride on him,
But! He will be in charge
Charging round the village green
A great white lolloping lump
When he pulls up outside my gate
I'll be thrown off with a bump
Now I'm beginning to sweat, oh thank God I've woken up
Cos there on his doggie cushion
Is my pure white Westie pup, 'Aah'
And Magic, because you never know when he'll appear
And never know where he'll disappear to
'Magic, Magic, where are you?'

Sandra Witt

Duzi And Shaka

Not just pets – but friends for life.
A rock through trouble, stress and strife.
If you are feeling low, they will bring joy
One's a girl and one's a boy
Duzi is our lady fair
Loves to steal your favourite chair
Shaka, he will let you know when he thinks it's time to go
He wants to 'frolic', wants to run
Over fields, have some fun
He lets you know it's time to start
Gets your attention with his bark.
Duzi bless her joins the fun
Throw her ball and off she runs
They fill my day with fun and joy
One's a girl and one's a boy.

Reg Giddings

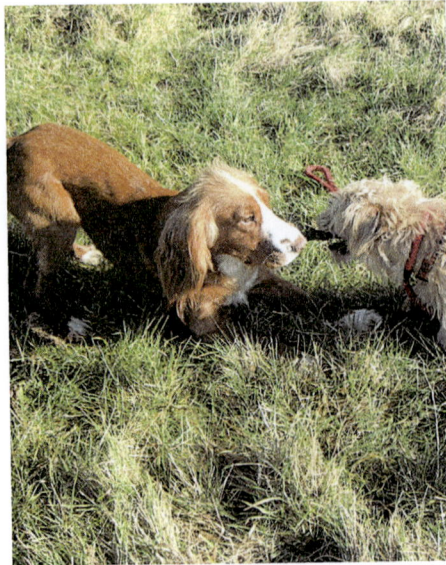

Pitkin

Let me introduce myself . . .
I'm Pitkin.
I'm very much a mummy's boy.
Cute and cuddly am I.
Playing chase
and fetching toys.
For you to throw for me.
I think nothing of
pinching the dog's food
Or teddies either.
Watch me as I run around the room.
Going 200 miles per minute!
Across the furniture I slide.
Before trying to stop.
Only to fall on my bottom.
When I'm being mischievous.
And someone's watching
Then with blue, doe-like eyes.
That seem to hypnotise you.
Your heart will melt.
Then I've got you . . .
Wrapped around my little paw.
Adventurous, nosing around in the cupboards.
And when you bring back shopping
I'm the first to smell out lunch . . .
Even if it's yours!
When I'm tired
You're a comfy lap or pillow for me
I'll even let you share my bed
So long as you don't
Take all the blanket . . .
That is!

Jessica Stephanie Powell

Mitzie And Jimmy The Handsome Twosome

I love and adore these two Daschunds so sweet and so fine
Scurrying around with their tiny feet in tune in time
Mitzie the princess with a face to match, with flair and prowess like no other little doggy
could match
Jimmy a gent the prince with a Mohican hair patch
Jimmy will follow Mitzie whatever she decides
Especially the stones she finds and hides.

The photo above speaks volumes how happy these doggies are
Mitzie and Jimmy come as a twosome and are rarely apart
Whenever their owners are away they will break their little hearts
Their owners care and look after these two so well and of course with their own antics to tell
Mitzie and Jimmy are guaranteed to shower you with welcomes galore
As you walk through their front door
Love and affection, strokes, tickles on their tums is what Mitzie and Jimmy crave
from everyone.

One could simply pass a day stroking and caring for my two furry friends
The love you get back in return is second to none
Who needs a human soul to connect with and love?
Just knowing Mitzie Witzie and Mohican Jim
Is Heaven sent from above
Both their cute faces could launch many ships
Their welcome is a welcome not to miss.

Marian Rosetta O'Reilly

What Am I?

Hey you look at me!
I'm Twtun ap Steffan
Can't you see . . . e me!

My favourite food is a small red chilli,
Monkeys shells and nuts,
As a treat – honey bar on a stick
I drink the same as a lion!
But if I eat avocado I'll die!

Amongst my hobbies I like to;
Ring the bell, chew colourful sticks
I also love to climb everywhere,
Anything, anywhere, anyhow,
But my favourite is upside down!

I swing on my colourful swing
Backwards and forwards
To the left and then the right
Faster and faster as a fleet of wind
And as soft as falling snow.

What else do I like doing?
I like to sing loudly,
Whistle even louder,
Have a bath in drinking water,
Then after, scratch my head!

Have you guessed yet what am I?
No!
I'll give you a clue!

I originally come from India's tropical rainforest
Where the climate is hot and humid.
I'm turquoise blue with a big red hooter
My legs are strong and thin
And my grip is like an eagle.

Have you guessed yet what I am?
Has the penny finally dropped?
Open the flap, then you'll see!
Yes that's right.
I'm a blue Indian ring neck parakeet!

Gwen Mared

The Tea Loving Parrot

With scalloped feathers around her neck,
And fiery tail, she's all bedecked,
To do a circuit in our room,
Then to my arm, she will zoom.

Pretty Purdie is her name,
Who enjoys much fun and game,
But there's one thing she likes to do,
And here I will explain to you.

When she wants to wet her whistle,
As her throat is dry as thistle,
'Purdie's cup of tea,' she conveys,
Oh how she loves those earl greys.

Tepid tea she likes to sup,
From a bone china cup,
Taps the side if it's too hot,
With her bill often or not.

Rocking and bobbing, full of glee,
Having had her cup of tea,
She chatters away, ten to the dozen,
She might well be my African cousin.

Gillian Balsdon

Fellow Travellers

When you are old, so many pets –
You have loved and lost and loved again.
Your memories of their times and ways
Now give you pleasure and a little pain
There was Tibby and Libby, two friendly cats
There was Mushti, my army canine
Mushti is Maltese for 'darling'
And he was a whole unit's darling and mine!

One of my sons kept a few tames rats –
They were intelligent and loving to mind
Then we had a mouse called Tommy
Who was apparently a saint of his kind!
There was Traddles who had three different addresses
There was Algie, who was next in line,
Followed by Pudding and Nelson
Nelson, poor chap, was almost blind.

We had a Border Collie called Jumble
Who, staying strictly true to his breed
Rounded up ladies on bicycles –
Which was something we did not need
We had a pet rabbit called Thumper
Who really thought he was a cat
He roamed the house, lolloped upstairs
And, when tired, he slept on my lap!

Then we took a rescue cat
She's Berry and is with us still
She was wild and in eight years is not much better
But we struggle on with a will.
In little ways she favours us
But, outsiders she cannot bear
Children are her worst nightmare
She runs from them (their visits are rare).

All of them had their own little ways
We loved them all in their day.
We look back with affection across the years
At the pets who helped us on our way!

Joyce M Jones

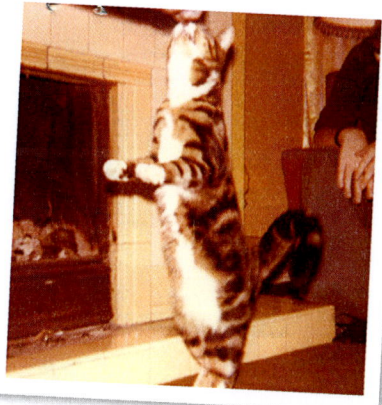

Lia Mia

Lia, our yellow-eyed, black kitten
Slept peacefully on the windowsill.
Until, the moment when Cyril Squirrel,
Came to the bird nut-feeder for his fill.

His heavy arrival banged the metal feeder
With a mighty crash against the windowpane.
Lia awoke startled, leapt up and turned to see,
A giant mouse? But that was just insane!

Feeding birds never troubled her
She would dab her tiny paws at them.
But this must be a case of long-term neglect.
An extremely serious mouse problem!

She stood up, stretched to her fullest height,
Scratched at the glass, showed the creature her teeth.
Cyril stared then growled at her, bared his long yellow fangs.
Startled, Lia reeled back, fell down to the floor beneath.

Her human called Mum, picked her up.
She comforted her, but only her dignity was hurt
She'd failed to scare a mouse, she felt less than a cat.
'Never mind,' Mum told her. 'You raised the alert.'

The one her family called Dad rushed out,
Filled Cyril with such alarm, that he ran for his life.
Lia tried to follow him out but, 'Your safer inside,' Dad said.
She was determined; someday she'd give Cyril strife.

Throughout autumn and winter Lia grew,
Found dozing before the fire better than being outside.
When awake she honed hunting skills, with her family's help.
That giant mouse would find no possible place to hide.

Spring arrived: Cyril was lured out from his dray.
Seeing him again at the feeder, angry Lia sprang at the glass.
He squealed as she soared toward him then startled fell to the ground.
The cat had grown, sleek and proud, to the top of her class!

Julie Freeborn

Tragedy

A little tragedy outside my window
Makes the silence of the evening
Scatter, the neighbours run outside
To see what is the matter.
And in the middle of the street
There lies a cat. A very quiet cat,
That fell out of a tree.

'He's dead,' so much is certain,
So much can now be said.
Some people cry, although this cat was stray
And not of theirs. After long debating,
A plastic bag is fetched, the cat is put in it
And everyone goes home.

The neighbour with the biggest heart
Carries the bag with due respect.
An hour later I look outside,
It is dark now. In the lantern light,
Something is moving, so I look twice,
To see what's going on:
A plastic bag is crawling down the street.

Yes, when you have nine lives to live,
You often land right on your feet.

Ina Schroders-Zeeders

Angel In Disguise

Here's what the butterflies
Out in the yard
Probably say about Chimpo:
Steer clear of that psycho
She'll tear you apart
With her sharp claws so you'd better
Not let her catch you off guard

Don't put yourself in danger
By fluttering anywhere near her
She may not have wings but she sure is agile
Fast on her feet and has good reach
With one quick leap, paws outstretched
That little wretch may just get her catch

The squirrels agree that Chimpo is trouble
When she's around, they cannot roam free
They scamper for cover and a safe hiding place
Not daring to even peep in case
They catch a glimpse of her frightening face

If one of them is not so lucky
And does not hurry enough to hide on time
He'll know he's been spotted
When she crouches low and wiggles her hind
Then she'll launch off like a rocket in pursuit of a target
While the poor squirrel scrambles in desperation
Hoping to outrun the abomination
Lest she pounces and tackles him to oblivion

While my mother doesn't quite think she's a monster
Chimpo does make her scream in horror
When she climbs up the curtains
To get to the lizard high up on the wall
Once, she barely avoided a hard fall
Pulling the curtain partially off its hook in the process
Claws tucked into the fabric, she dangled precariously
While my mother yelled at her angrily

Me? I have no problem with Chimpo
Not even when her head suddenly
Pops up above my knees
When I've propped them up
To support the book I'm reading
After that, she'll climb over my knees
To settle herself on my lap
Ignoring the fact that I'm reading
She'll take a nice long nap

Chimpo may leave many in exasperation
But I see no malice in her actions
Her big bright eyes shine with excited innocence
She may be a handful but my cat is no fiend
All Chimpo just wants is to have some fun
Full of passion and enthusiasm
Comes galloping like a gazelle when called

Her face so earnest and sweet
When she starts to knead
Some part of my body as I am falling asleep
When she's done, curls up against me
Warm and cuddly, so adorable
To me, she's absolutely an angel.

Najua Ismail

Tiger

Creeping through the bushes,
On the hunt again,
On the trail of some poor spider,
Or an imaginary threat.
The wind makes you jump,
A dog's bark makes you squat,
Twilight makes you crazy and wild,
You're a fearless hunter as well as a pet.
Mewing on the windowsill,
All attention to get in,
Distracted all of a sudden to preen
Your fur again.
I own a little tiger, stripes, purrs and claws,
Snoozing by the fireside worn out from the prowl.

Paula Elizabeth Redmond

Across The Great Divide

A million miles from here
I remember, wide open spaces
Endless blue skies, I was clear
No cares – only life's little graces
And the natives to revere.

Upon your bare back I rode – racing
As if I had somewhere to go
Holding onto your red mane – blowing
In the wind, over plateaus
Onto life's rocky course – advancing

I can still smell your sweat
And see your mouth foam –
Your handsome silhouette
Together we roamed
Across the great divide

Time has not marred memory
Nor altered youth's affection
Though long gaps are delusory
With this picture of perfection
When we were a reality.

Carla Iacovetti

The Jackals Of Mayo Road

Yellow glebe cooling,
Banyan leaves crackling,
Flies buzzing and
The boundary wall fading.

Snouts emerge from
The blind well burrows
Testing crepuscular instinct
For another summer champ.

At midnight birds in
The hencoop cluck aloud
To the pack's failed blitz,
Startled stray dogs yelp.

After the silence a bewailing cry
From the junkyard fence
Huti-huwao-huwao-huwao,
Huti-huti huwao-huwao-huwao!

Mukesh Williams

Nature

Deep in the canyon
Sole coyote's crying laugh
Danger impending

Coyotes lurking
Sad mystical miscreants
Song dogs of the wild.

Diana Kwiatkowski Rubin

Rusty

The gaze of unconditional love
Stares from those deep set eyes.
As black as a sooty raven's wing,
As serene as a cloud-strewn sky.
With endearing looks of expectancy,
He wags his bottle-brush tail.
He knows it's time for 'walkies',
An indisputable alpha male.

In Himley Woods, his favourite jaunt,
He romps with unbridled glee.
Splashing in the swamp, barking at the birds,
Or sniffing at a silver birch tree.
But when alarmed, he expands his chest,
Leonine stance defensive.
Postman, strangers, garbage collectors,
They're on his list of offensives.

An air of aristocratic nonchalance
Depicts his blue blood race.
His ruff, a halo of dense copper tufts
Frames his teddy bear face.
Being very selective about his peers,
He acknowledges only blondes.
Hence, the foxy grin and excitable pant
Plus a slurp from the bluish black tongue.

His hindquarters we've named 'trousers',
Grooming has become a nightmare.
Coaxing him with titbits of ham or cheese,
His resistance made my Mom swear.
Due to his autonomous spirit,
Dog training classes were futile,
He behaved like a roguish lothario,
Disobedient and certainly not docile.

He's rolled around in fox droppings,
Is partial to horse manure.
Sweaty feet or smelly socks,
A good bath is the only cure.
Our watchdog par excellence,
Rumbustious, russet red Chow.
He has a loyal heart of gold,
And only he knows how.

Jill Pisani

Elephant Fort

Black beauties in chains –
Before the ticket counters,
A long queue does creep
To scatter near the black wonders.

Ears and tails always move,
Ruminating the rhythms of forest.
Elephants are inside the fort,
Exposed to the sky barest.

I hear the hushed emotions
In the clinking of chains.
Hearts smoulder in;
Eyes emit lava of pains.

Burning red wild flowers
And tickling streams
Each elephant longs I know:
But dreams die in chains.

Fabiyas M V

The Pet I Never Had

Monkeys have
No manners or graces
They embarrass themselves
In public places

They eat their food
With fingers and thumbs
They use their hands
To scratch their bums

They swing from bars
All day in cages
Gnashing their teeth and
Going bananas.

James Tierney

Sweet Little Benji

Sweet little Benji
He gives Tiffany a bone
And they are now friends.

Laraine Smith

Caged Beauty

His jungle is somewhere green
And breathing beauty full of horror,
All days seem there heated roarer,
All nights are frozen by spleen.

The little parrot is from there,
A feathered lemon with sharp claws,
He feels completely at a loss
With no songs in fragrant air,

In spite of having corn enough,
With no wind and heavy rain,
All things are not to be complained,
And my green eyes are full of love.

He's fallen in a lemon sorrow
And gently formed with wings an angle,
In tiny eyes I see the jungle
Still breathing beauty of the morrow.

Natalia Gorodova

Animal Antics

I like Robert, my cat
His fur is shaggy and his belly is fat
He lies in the sun and waits all day,
To catch little critters that pass his way.
He isn't a killer, he's just taking his chances,
Close to the ground as his claw advances,
Towards a lizard, a frog, a shrew or a mouse,
They're toys for his playtime or lunch on the house.

Gillian Sewell

Cuddles And Nuggets

Ere my spirit expire vitiated,
Tick clock tick but tick anti-clockwise,
Undeflower me back to the days of my virgin eyes,
And once again let me feel those sensations that animated in my mind;
Those of memories so sweet, simple and kind;
Of a romance my aged years have come to revere,
Reminiscent through the eye of this room;
As they canoodle under the bliss of a celestial sky
And leave their apparitions embalmed in the womb of a beaming moon,
Since now sensibility has found its votaries, and for gallantry to reign supreme:
Buk, buk, bukkaaa and cluck, cluck I do they vow!
For what else in this world is still of matter anymore?
But their fraternity of love that bloomed past springs;
And in the Ark of comfort, solidified their union.

Nyakallo Joy Moeketsi

65

The Cat Lady

Hermione Handcart, sixty-three, had horrid breath and one bad knee,
of seven husbands two were dead, the other five had up and fled;
But each left homes and pots of cash, and H possessed of quite a stash.
so now Hermione rented flats, and lived alone – with thirteen cats.

Three tabby toms and one black she, a Russian Blue she got for free,
an Abyssinian with big ears, a racing cat with eighteen gears;
The fattest ginger tom you've seen, a Siamese pair called 'King' and 'Queen',
a tortoiseshell with wonky knees and two grey strays with shocking fleas.

Her visitors were far and few, for fur and fleas and trays of poo,
abounded each and every room, within the claw-scratched curtained gloom;
Where every cushion had a cat, and tabby toms wee'd in your hat,
or used your legs to sharpen claws, and yowled and screeched with bare a pause.

The 'racing' cat she christened 'Fizz', around each room in turn would whizz,
at just head high across the walls, the loo, the kitchen, and the halls;
In search of heads left just so near; to passing, rake, about the ear,
just pausing once, on each third lap, to give the ginger tom a slap.

The tortoiseshell, three left, two right, would wobble, more or less upright,
'fore bumping into legs of chairs, or pitching headlong down the stairs;
And catapulting from his bed, old big ears on the seventh tread,
as claws outstretched and knees awry, the tortoiseshell went bouncing by.

The Russian Blue, a bolshie mog, who'd come off worse with fourteen's dog,
sits glaring now beneath your seat, just darting out to bite your feet;
Or in the shadows lurks, all sly, with half a tail, one ear, one eye,
while 'King' and 'Queen' strut smug about; or give the ginger tom a clout.

The world's best mouser, coal-black she, would hide them under the settee,
along with squirrels, frogs and rats, and hedgehogs, slow worms, toads and bats;
With some deceased and others not, which out from 'neath the settee shot,
the feral greys named 'Pitch' and 'Patch', did nothing much but sit and scratch!

The postman left the mail next door, and swore she'd not make sixty-four,
for when he'd popped the mail slot flap, a bunch of claws shot out the gap;
And there Hermione lived and died, with thirteen cats still by her side,
behind the purple painted door, upon the very topmost floor.

Sullivan the Poet

Cat Burglar

There are many happy kittens who live here in our block
And all can come and visit me cos my cat flap's got no lock.
They're in and out both night and day, no privacy for me.
I wish they'd find another home from which to nick their tea.
The food I leave for later on is never there for long
And when I feel the need to eat I find that it's all gone.
I don't know who the villain is but have some good ideas.
She's ginger and she lives next door and has done so for years.
So Tiffy if I catch you miss, I'll stand for it no more,
As very soon you'll surely find there's a lock upon my door.
Electro-magnet is the key so I can live in peace,
And from then on I hope to find the nicking then will cease.
No matter how you wail and scratch, miaow or scream or shout
The door will never open 'till it's me who's coming out.
Yes one fine day I promise you, you'll get the biggest shock.
For when you come a calling you'll find I've got my lock.

Ruth Laughton

Roots The Cat

Young Roots, he is a mariner cat,
A prideful captain, he;
At the bow of the ship he sits with a smile
As his shipmates put to sea.

What wondrous lands will he view today?
What strange things will he find,
As he sails the oceans of the world
And leaves his home behind?

His ship is but a rowboat small,
Our family is his crew;
The sea is the lake beside our home,
But not in our captain's view.

When he sees us starting for the boat,
He quickly jumps aboard,
And positions himself at the very bow;
Our laughter quite ignored.

For Roots, he is a mariner cat,
A prideful captain, he;
At the bow of the ship he sits with a smile
As his shipmates put to sea!

John Bliven Morin

Game, Set, Match . . .

First, there is a game of rounders,
Chasing fast, batting the ball.
Football is next in order of play
(A win for the 'Blues'?)
Oh no, it's a draw!

Then – they run ahead –
To stand side by side at the starting line –
Ready, steady, go . . .
Heads down – the race has started –
They glance sideways at each other
To catulate – sorry – calculate –
Who is ahead?
Who is nearer the finish line?
Soon reached – a draw?

They look at each other – and sniff
So it is time for a wrestling match –
Their legs wrap round each other,
They tumble, twist and turn on the floor –
Another draw. Game over – or is it?

Sort of –
For now it is time to play cat and mouse –
Mum says 'But I wanted to play with
My mouse mew – sorry – now'
Then catipulates – sorry – capitulates.
As they look with eyes that beguile
The mice appear – they flick their ears!
They grin at each other – like a Chelsea – sorry – Cheshire cat!
Every one's a winner they seem to say – climbing onto her lap.
(They sense she needs to sit and rest for a while!)
'We've got her just where we want her,
Right beneath our paws!'
They smile at each other their secret smile –
Purring to their heart's content . . .

Anita Richards

My Best Friend, Gannet
(Dedicated to my cat who returned to me after 2 years of being missing)

My best friend is fantastic
She always makes me laugh
She would go ballistic
At the thought of taking a bath

My best friend sleeps so cutely
She is absolutely the sweetest thing
Being with her doesn't feel like a duty
And when she comes to my room, I always let her in

My best friend always knows my mind
When I'm upset, she comes by my side
She accompanies me, just to be kind
And in the darkness she is a radiant guide

My best friend isn't like 'false' friends at school
I can trust her with any secret
She doesn't call me names when I act the fool
To me she's much more than a pet

My best friend can never be fake
Because she does not know deceit or spite
She is a free feline, not an evil snake
It's a shame dark 'friends' don't emit her light

My best friend shares a bond of mutual affection
She constantly shows it
We maintain a reciprocal connection
Everyone who sees us knows it

My best friend's stunning, sleek and sinuous
I thank God for her each day, she probably doesn't know
My love and blessings for her are continuous
I pray she will never mislay her soft glow.

Rochelle Logan-Rodgers

Two Animals In Conversation

Nan: Good morning Billy, it's half-past eight
Your breakfast will soon be ready
But don't try and jump over the gate
Or you could end up being someone's teddy

Billy: It's OK Nan, I'll stay nice and calm
I'll stand next in line to you
I wonder if there will be pieces on jam
Or anything sweet will do

Nan: Well Billy, take care son
When the children come to play
Because they are full of tricks and fun
And they'll try to chase you away

Billy: I can stand up for myself, Nan
Said Billy with a grin
If the children come near me, Nan
I'll just kick them on the chin

Nan: Oh no, Billy, you can't be cruel
You cannot flip your lid
Your grandad was a famous fool
Once known as Billy the Kid

Billy: It's alright, Nan, Billy said
With a cheeky grin on his face
Last night Grandad shared my bed
And asked me to take his place

Nan: Well Billy, you can do what you must
But there's something you must note
If you kick a child for the sake of a crust
Then you too are a silly old goat.

Lynda Johns

Paddy With Soul

Just like me, Paddy has a soul,
I saw it in his eyes,
When it peeped to stare at mine,
It was mellow
And had a halo
And winked at mine in utter glee.

Now our souls are the best of mates
Who will never be apart.
Mine is in my heart
But his at his feet.
Feet that run for my amusement.
Feet that run to my protection.

Just like most days, we look at the stars.
As Paddy counts them with every blink and swish of tail,
I know our wish upon them is the same . . .
That our days together may be as many
As that abundance above,

Now still I say . . . Paddy has a soul.
I saw it in his eyes
When it peeped to stare at mine.
Now our souls are the best of mates
Who will never be apart.

Zinzile Mngomezulu

Missie The Bedspring

A Bedlington and Springer cross,
Missie is her name,
We had her from a puppy,
She drove us quite insane,
Now she is four years old,
We would not be without her,
And thank God it was her we chose,
As the husband wanted her brother,
Hour long walks in the park,
Playing with her ball,
When she brings it back to you,
You feel ten foot tall,
Her tail wags all day long,
She is a happy sight,
But if she sees a fly or bee,
She will run away in fright,
She is the world's greatest dog,
I tell her all the time,
I really am quite privileged,
She chooses to be mine.

Sara Baker

Pushka - An Elegy

The little Russian doll
was called Babushka
The name was evocative
of my pal Pushka

It was an austere autumn night
when Pushka arrived as a tiny black waif
ensconced in a shoebox
with a half smile on his face

Pushka blossomed, became an Adonis
as svelte as a Siamese
More handsome than Ramses
always at ease

He adored the Victorian garden
chilling out on the sunny lawn
Stalking unwary birds and mice, sadly
often to be slain!

Pushka had a penchant
for prime halibut or turbot
from Waitrose in Finchley Road
Oh! What we do for love!

However, at sixteen, Pushka became ill,
was so utterly miserable
Brendan the vet, said it would be kinder
for my dear mate to enter into sleep

I lovingly dug Pushka's gave
in the garden, where he had been so happy
When I took the last look
Pushka had a half smile on his face

Donald McDonnell

Katie

We had a lovely cockatiel. Katie was her name,
My daughter Jenny managed to get her finger tame.
By and by our Katie got a little bolder
Climbed from Jenny's finger and settled on her shoulder.
Then one day she just took off – flew right across the room
Settled on my shoulder and nearly met her doom.
I'd added washing up liquid to water in the sink.
On impulse she took off again, I had no time to think.
Bubbles are not safe at all for little birds to land.
She sank! Of course I yanked her out. She sat there on my hand
Sopping wet and spluttering. She looked a sorry sight.
The thought that she had nearly drowned gave us quite a fright.
I didn't want to scare her, but thought I'd have a try
At speeding up the process of getting Katie dry.
The radiator was quite warm, and so I put her there
Upon a towel the children fetched and then spread out with care.
We got the hairdryer, plugged it in, but didn't stand too near
In case the dreadful noise of it filled Katie with fear.
She absolutely loved it and spread her wings out wide
Then turned around as if to say, 'Now dry me on this side!'

Josephine Price

The Chase
(For Fizz)

Blue ball bounces across cluttered room,
Flash of red fur, dog crashes to doom.
Nails scratch across tiles; rip over floor,
As soggy wet object squashes into the door.
Red, warm tornado hurtles through the chairs,
As object of chase rebounds off the stairs,
Sharp jaws snap shut, the ball has been taken!
Molars grind and scrap as the ball is shaken.
A tiny bell rings out, in plaintive sound,
As deep-throated growl, surges through hound.
He lies on fat belly, four paws by his side,
Tail beating happily, jaws open wide.
The grating sound ends and the ball rolls away,
While dog flops onto his side, tired of play.
The savage ball chaser is curled on the rug;
A moment of peace in the life of a pug!

Rainbow Reed

Tuffy The Terrier Who Told Terrible Tales

My Tuffy the terrier told many tales
And teased the old Toozala bird
He'd twist on the tides and laugh at the moon
And never he'd tell a true word!

Two Tuesdays ago, old Tuffy was spied
By the wily old Toozala bird
Appearing to totter in trouble transfixed
So the Toozala swooped undeterred!

Tuffy the terrier (who told many tales)
Cried: 'I'm perched on an old flowerpot!
And when the tide turns, old Toozala, dear
I shall drown and be all but forgot!'

Tweeted the Toozala: 'Tuffy, old chap!
I suspect that you *swim* – on the spot!
And when the tide turns, old Tuffy, old man!
Your claims will be proved tommyrot!'

Tuffy the terrier mused to himself
'That Toozala's wiser than I!
For I'm chilly and dank
– What a silly old prank!
I think I'll trot home and get dry!'

'Barley' Robinson

Harvey

Sweet dear doggy, light of my life,
How you do so brighten my days
With wiggles, wags and welcome grins
And in so many other silly ways.

So I will always know what you wish of me,
You have a myriad of clever vocal ways.
Barks and squeaks and moans and growls,
Your repertoire, an opera diva would amaze.

No matter what *you* decide that we must do,
Whether to rise early, sleep late, go out or stay in,
Your joyous exuberance propels every venture.
Just so it's not a trip to the dreaded veterinarian.

Your favourite occupation is certainly walkies
Where clearly you engage in a mock hunt event.
As your cruise the territory for any signs;
Your nose is twitching: surveillance by scent.

Pursuit promises reward is the canine creed.
Sound words or so it seemed on this quest I now relate.
You spied the quarry through the shop window glass.
Poor unsuspecting velvet octopus knew not his fate.

Did you think to ignore the windowpane?
Hot pursuit robbed your reason I guess,
For you rushed forward and crashed head first
And knocked yourself fairly senseless.

The shopkeeper heard the thump and thud
And rushed out front to give her aid.
You stood stunned and unsteady on your paws,
Not knowing the mistake you'd made.

The lady disappeared inside then right out again,
Clutching the pink and blue-legged toy squid.
'Twas the very one you'd aimed your sights upon
And now she offered it to you. Yes she did!

Snatching the beast in the blink of an eye,
Scrunching and crunching your captured prey,
While it mysteriously emits aquatic squeaks,
You quickly forget the price you'd paid.

We two ladies could not help but giggle,
For your gusto at the 'kill' amused us no end
And once again, I love you for your funny side
Plus, I'm sure your wee brow will mend.

Isolde Nettles MacKay

Puppy Love

I didn't choose you,
You chose me,
On that first day,
That I came to see,
You and your siblings,
Playing so free.

At first you all seemed,
Much like the rest,
Big, beautiful and chunky
Happy and playful, the best!

But then I saw you,
Being cheeky and bright,
And then you saw me,
And your face became a light,
With a joy and a wonder rarely seen,
And look of accusation as to where I had been.

Like you had been waiting
Especially for me.
I felt very important,
In that single second there,
As you wiggled and squirmed and gave a deep stare.

I knew my life had been waiting for you,
And yours has been waiting just for me too!
You looked so happy; I felt deep love inside;
Echoed beneath in your deep brown eyes.

You ran straight to my side
And demanded a cuddle
Followed me around,
And got close for a huddle.

I knew there and then, that all the others I had seen,
Just could no longer compare,
And when I left the first time, I felt really mean,
And I know it didn't seem fair,
But inside I felt it and I could see,
All the others hadn't been right,
Because you were the right one for me!

You tried to follow me,
But you couldn't come yet,
But I would see you soon,
On that you could bet.

I left my heart there,
And took yours with me,
I was only showing I cared,
So soon one day, we could be,
Forever together,
Just you and me!

And when I came back,
You remembered me!
And without having a moment to think,
You were wrapped around my legs, before I could blink,
So I took you home,
Where you will stay,
Forever with me,
Happy together,
For eternity.

Zoe Davis

Dylan

You were taken from this world too soon Dylan
Just a kitten, only two years old.
A can crushed while many ml of life remained inside
A sapling destroyed
A caterpillar savaged by the carnivorous bird of tragedy.

That old saying 'curiosity killed the cat' bears brutal truth
His lust for exploring entangled with murderous car wheels
To cause his cruel and untimely demise.

When Dylan didn't come home we waited up.
We simply suspected that he'd embarked on another midnight adventure.
Not this time; as hour after hour passed, panic set in forcefully
Where was he?
What had happened?
Was he hurt?

We soon spread word of his disappearance
Frantically increasing the search party as we desperately tried to rescue him.

Finally news came; news but no relief
Our neighbour found him
Crying in the field behind our house
A wounded soldier dragging his broken bones
Desperately battling to make it home,
Dried blood clinging to his soft fur;
His body weak with exhaustion

'Damaged tissue and shattered bone in two legs,' the vet said.
To put him to sleep was the kindest thing.
I stroked him gently; tear drops forming in my eyes.
Gradually his body became limp and sleepy, till at last he was still.

It's many years since Dylan died but he lives on, forever not forgotten,
In the playground of childhood memories.

I remember how his favourite toy was a rolled up paper ball;
How he loved to dribble it across the hall.
How when he slept on the bed with his legs stretched ahead it looked rather like
he was praying.
How he liked to jump in my doll's pushchair and have me wheel him around

Dylan, kitten, you were such a character
If they have cat comedians in pet heaven I know you'll be doing me proud.

RIP – I'll never forget you.

Maisie Buckley

MeMe

From whence MeMe came a mystery for sure
Our b&b, feline foible of fur
She-me's a he-me, our adopted sole stray
Checked out the joint and opted to stay
Prints muddy paws on washed rucked up mat
Does our mischievous, devious big burly cat

With enviable ease onto wooden ledge springs
Content rumbling purr at loud volume rings
Veiled in net like a newlywed bride
In sunny windowsill sits bird watching outside
With a nonchalant swish of his tortoiseshell broom
Arched skeletal stretch, stately sweeps across room

Tendency to swipe with a temperamental streak
Law unto himself, forbidden places to sneak
He's headstrong, stubborn, a real scaredy-puss
Disappears under table, the mere hint of a fuss
Into infinity roams our wandering 'Me'
But one thing I know he'll be home for his tea.

Shirley Clayden

My Proud Cat

My cat still rules this neck of the woods
Walking through the garden paths
And the green grass of snails and ladybirds
He's got whiskers cute and a smile to boot
He eats a satisfying meal, night and day
Hunts the birds that stray to his claws
He's smarter than most and knows what to do
He's proud to be a free spirit all subtle dreams
Of flowers and grass and fulfilling things
Of lying in the sun where the feel is heavenly
And I adore him more than life and nine lives.

Muhammad Khurram Salim

Dog-Handler And His Dog

Here boy, stay. Sleep quietly by my side.
Here in the peace, stretch out and take your rest.
Our war is over; others take our place on broken streets.
There, on that may-filled afternoon
In one great painless glare of light
We died.
They took our lives, but could not take our love;
That lay beyond the bloody reach of war.

Here boy, stay. Sleep quietly by my side.
Soon we shall hear the captain call our names
And we shall rise.
Together we shall see Him who created us,
And walk with Him the golden streets
Where no war is,
Where we may walk in safety
And in peace.

Robert Brown

A Groomer's Tale

Bobby needs a haircut,
He can't see a thing.
There's a bit of a whiff from his butt,
So, I thought I should ring.

He has knots in his skirt
And his claws need a trim.
His coat is full of dirt,
I know it sounds a bit grim.

I love him to look like a puppy,
So don't clip him too short.
A cute round head, and all fluffy,
As it needs to hide his wart.

The family are coming to stay,
What time do you shut?
It's a bit short notice, can you do him today?
Bobby really needs a haircut.

Jane Cope

A Cat's Life

High above your loving eyes I wonder why you stare
Majestically you turn your head and leave without a care
You saunter out to where you'll lie and nestle in a ball
I call your name, it's just a sound; you're master after all

Yet when the bowl is looking bare I'm never left alone
The purring trance you radiate is comforting in tone
Behind the mask I know your interests really lie elsewhere
Far from me to turn you down, you've played your mind games fair

Such childlike nature you possess, and yet you dare to roam
Searching for another place to call your second home
Making friends along the way to call upon at night
Living out your predatory dreams that bring you such delight

You've touched my heart without a thought of what I mean to you
A feline trait that's always been and continues its way through
Nonetheless I hold you tight to keep you warm and safe
Peering up you squint at me and try to stay awake

I admire the way you live your life and do the things you do
Strolling through the land you own, returning for your food
I'll be there to watch you grow and play when you're around
You've spoken words of love to me, without a single sound.

Daniel Conner

and the good things that once were

Whenever I pat him
I'm taking him back to cosy times
with his mum.

He rubs up against my arm, nudges my hand
with his head, prompts me into action

OK, Leicester

I rub the back of his neck
and the purring begins in earnest

something down the backyard
distracts me

and Leicester reminds me
why I'm here

and nudges my hand.

OK, Leicester

I watch his eyes relax once again and close slowly
as I stroke his neck.

he sits there like a little man with head bowed
and thinks of childhood

and the good things
that once were.

Brad Evans

The Terrier With Tourette's

A familiar story, a tough early start as a pet shop product of a broken home
She lived a tin-can life of wheelie bins, refuge trucks and collectors
In reflective jackets and kick boots, she had run away to be free
To be snatched by a Dog Warden on a Salford street
A Parson's Jack Russell never could be
A match for a noose and pole

For a time in a rescue centre pen, she pined, not for company but for the open road
To be tail-up and ready to run, not to be behind bars but to be under stars
She would curl up into a puppy ball, withdrawn and lost
To the barking cacophony of her fellow inmates
In a psychiatric ward Bedlam for dogs
They needed to find a home

Then Patty came here but even the clip clop of horses common to rural roads
Turned her flight-fight on when she swore in screams of barks and growls
She screamed at sheep and other dogs or people lacking social skills
And switched from Dr Dog Jekyll to Mrs Dog Hyde
Changing from play to home-alone howls
Until she found her calm.

David Sands

Untitled

Everything's harder now
The smiles, the laughter –
The facade
I used to hoist up that white smile
As I would a white sail against a cyan blue sky
And then bask in the sunlight of other's reflected rays
I used to
Now though
People exhaust me with their endless
Questions
I'd rather drift past with my grey, worn sail
Down, and surrender to the current instead
I'm weary; I'm driftwood
But I have you, my friend to pick me up gently in your mouth
You, whose love is so easily bought
With food but retained only with
Love
In return
Whose smile is not merely
A scenting of my pheromones
But concern
No need to pretend
To fake, or grin back
You can tell when I'm tired
So tired, I just want to curl up and –
Feel your warmth against me
A reassurance with each deep breath you take that
I am not alone
Because sometimes all I need is
Silence
And another being's warmth
Sometimes all I need is
You.

Ailsa Fineron

Narcissus

Watching your reflection –
It's a sign of who you are.
A puddle of clear water
Is your brightly shining star.
Watch me now immortalise you,
Watch me make your name,
In black and white, you're famous
So it's true that cats are vain.

Rachel Robins

The Day You Came

Six weeks old and in need of a home
Faced with the streets, a place to roam

Lost and alone and looking for love
You came to me – almost from above

Those big brown eyes and cute little face
That longing look made my heart race

Building a bond that no one could break
Inspiring my life that could only make

Happiness forever until you go
Living on in my heart so that you know

How much Harvey's life was meant to be
The little black dog that chose only me.

Jennifer Hyland
(Harvey the lifestyle dog®)

MacBeenz MacSquee

MacBeenz MacSquee is no ordinary cat
He's cunning and quick
He's lean (not fat).
MacBeenz MacSqee is a ninja in training.
Whiskers alert, muscles constraining
The heart of a lion residing within
The form of a tiger – the fur and the skin.
Exploring the bedroom
He's fearless and fleet.
Better watch out – he loves bare feet!
Ready to pounce on an unwary toe
Under the duvet, nothing on show.
But when it's 'lights out' he's up for a snoozle
Snuggling down, asleep like a woozle.
Twitching and quivering, the ninja breaks free
The fierce – The magnificent
MacBeenz MacSquee!

Sue Pattie

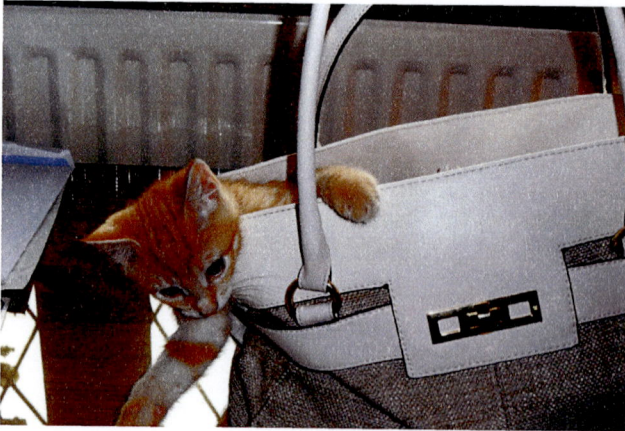

My Lurcher, Ice

All the way to Castleford we travelled one day
To view a fawn boy who had been left astray
The gypsies had left him hungry and alone
All he wanted was a place to call home

When we arrived his eyes were so sad
Which made me wonder what kind of life he had had?
I fell in love and knew he'd be OK
He just needed a little TLC every day

Slowly he grew into a real brave boy
Everything he did, he did it with joy
He would run like the wind through fields, across moors
It seemed like he didn't touch down with his paws

He became a real character, his confidence grew
He learnt to do tricks and he'd kiss if asked to!
Every day he was such a pleasure to own
He was my shadow, he made me feel so un-alone

For 15 good years he was my best mate
I never thought a relationship could ever be so great
But such as life is, he began to get weak
He would run a lot less and get much more sleep

He deteriorated more as he got old
His legs they failed him, he was tired and felt cold
The angels have been now and taken him away
I'm going to miss him so much, each and every day

His legs will be fixed now and he can run again
He won't be suffering or feeling any more pain
In his field of dreams is where he will be
Running, playing, absolutely free

So many people loved him it's hard to comprehend
I'll never forget you, Ice, my best friend.

Good night.

Tracy Kerr

Bo The Boa

Henry Oldfield, seven years old, tried to teach his snake to kill when told,
His mother thought it wasn't proper, and called her son down for his supper.
When Henry returned he practiced with Bo, the name he'd been given a week ago,
Henry tempted him with mice, the teasing something Bo found not nice.
Bo preferred to simply lay, under his heat lamp he spent his day.
One day after being teased really quite enough, Bo ate Henry while he was busy with army men and stuff,
He coiled and slunk to where Henry lay, then leapt and ate him while he was ready to play.
Henry's mother fell and received a nasty cut, after seeing her child in his own snake's gut,
She lamented the boy's loss but had to agree, for such cruel behaviour there ought to be a fee.
A lesson learned and a snake well fed, remember this children when you're in your bed;
Animals should be treated with care, or one day you may find yourself not there.

Hayley Rowe

In Memory Of Ebony

Your summer days are over
In amongst the flowers
Where you spent your
Time, to while away the hours
Your spirit now remains
In thoughts that we hold dear
As time drifts along
It is all so very clear.
That thou an enigmatic feline
You inspired a word or two
And several painted pictures
With Inky whom friendship grew.
Ebony we miss your attempted miaows
And your lovely golden eyes
You seemed so very distant
But you looked so very wise.
Inky is now lonesome
After so very many years,
We hope to see her sparkle
Now there are no more shedded tears.

Joyce Gale

Baby Boy

I can't believe how quickly time has passed and that it's coming up to a year,
Since I lost you baby boy – and everything that I held so dear.
Nearly a year since that fateful day, when my world came crashing down,
The day I lost my everything and my best friend was no longer around.
I can't forget the way you left and how much pain you must have been in that day,
And my feelings of hopelessness and despair, having to stand and watch you slip away.
To see your lifeless body on the table and to have to say goodbye,
Walking away and leaving you was the single hardest thing of my life.
Returning home without my boy, surrounded by all of your gear,
Desolation consumed me completely as I screamed for you to be here.
My house was no longer a home, without my baby by my side,
And without my precious angel, I had an existence and not a life.
I can still remember the anguish, because every day I feel the pain,
Of losing my very special man, and I know I'll suffer all over again.
When the day of 4th October arrives and I relive each painful minute,
And wishing it hadn't happened and that my life still had you in it.
I'd give anything for just an hour, to meet on Rainbow Bridge,
To hold you close and tell you how very much you're missed.
But how thankful I am for my angel, who taught me more than he'll ever know,
How grateful I am that he found me and rescued me from myself.
Who completed me and made me whole, whose cuddles were always there,
Who I could rely upon completely to always love and always care.
My baby boy, Albert-Jack, I miss you more than words can ever say,
But I know that we'll be together again, one very special day.

Lucy Barton

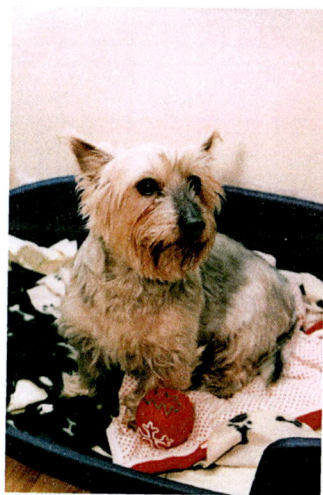

If I Were A Cat

If I were a cat
I would sleep all day
I would purr and purr
And never would stray

I would help catch mice
And drink lots of milk
I would lick my fur
So it felt like silk

I would be kind and true
And miaow and miaow
I would open doors
And never would scowl

If I were a cat
I would sleep all day
I would purr and purr
And never would stray.

Anne-Marie Large

Inquisitive

My precious angels are my children
They hold me together, they're my Zen
Big one is clever; watches the news
Greets Nan outside, she is like a guard dog
Small one likes kisses; and to air her views
She explores the outside world, traveller's mog
Big one's mute, slowly finding her voice
Sometimes cold, but often bringing me rejoice
Stroked and petted by their paws, their toy
Niftily digging their claws in, I'm a pin
Cushion and a cosy pillow as they lie
Dreaming of their daily jaunts, did they sin?
When awake they're stern with each other
But they'll watch out for one another.

Angela Moore

Robertson Is

Robertson is a farm cat
A barn cat
A mouses run for cover cat

Robertson is a chancer
A prancer
The leader of the dancer

Robertson is a stubby cat
A grubby cat
A roller in the dusty cat

Robertson is a prowler
A howler
An on the roof miaowler

Robertson is a crazy cat
A lazy cat
A snuggle on a cushion cat

Robertson is a bouncer
A flouncer
An on the mouse pouncer

Robertson is a needy cat
A greedy cat
A muncher of furry crunchies cat

Robertson is a lumper
A plumper
A heavy footed stumper

Robertson just is!

Alexander Hamilton

Millie

Millie's on the war-path;
Millie's on the prowl;
She twitches but a whisker;
She utters not a growl.

Robin's in the tree-top,
Ready poised for flight;
Wren is in the bushes,
Keeping out of sight.

Millie's sleek and tabby,
With fur as soft as silk;
Green eyes so mild and limpid
When asking for her milk.

Millie's on the war-path,
Those eyes so round and green
– How fierce! How terrifying
By tiny creature seen!

She twitches but a whisker;
She barely moves the grass;
But many sense her creeping,
And hide to let her pass.

Millie's like the roses,
So beautiful is she,
And yet as sharp as briars
Those claws of hers can be.

Millie's on the war-path,
Mouse, he has not seen
How soft she steals upon him
With eyes so bright and green.

Millie's creeping closer;
Robin safely sings;
But Mouse, he has not seen her
– And Mouse, he has no wings.

Mouse, he has not seen her,
Mouse, he has no wings;
She crouches lower, lower
– And suddenly she springs.

Jacqueline Ives-Ward

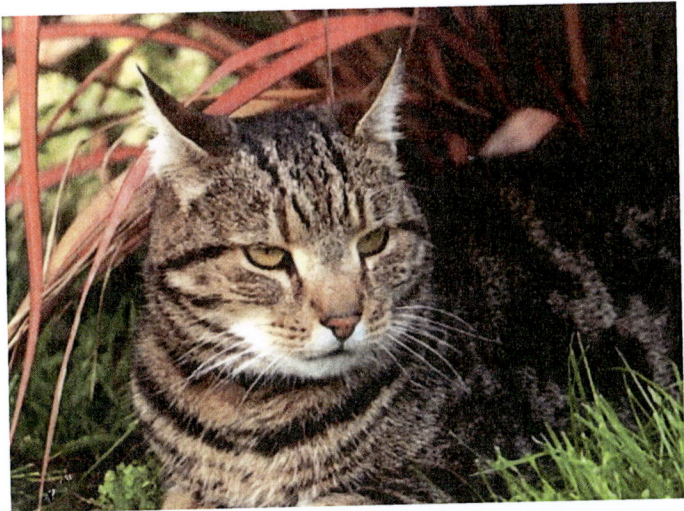

My Pet Dobermans

My Doberman pets that sit by my feet
Large, muscular, slender and neat
One with a shiny coat of black and tan
Mysty she's my number one fan
Loyal, obedient to a point
She obeys commands to a soft and gentle voice
Smart but a comic with her antics in mind
She's the leader of the two you will find
She's the one who makes you laugh
The funniest by half
The other Doberman Dee Dee, she's clever in many ways
All fawn in colour the one that plays
Talks and answers in return
But she's not too quick to learn
A little gentler and not so rough
It's her sister Mysty who is tough
Dobermans may look nasty and mean
But that's a rumour that's obscene
They are gentle and loving clowns
And good with infants to have around
As is said it's not the dog, it's the owner
And to do with the way they are treated more over
My girls as I call them to me are more than pets
Members of my family, I have no regrets
I treat them with respect, as they do in return
I think all together we live and learn.

Terry John Powell

DJ

My dog Dj is all about having fun
Especially when it's in the sun
He runs round the garden chasing bumblebees
Stopping every so often to do his wees
He looks so happy
One cute little chappy
As he runs with speed
And munches on the weeds
We try to teach him the best we can
But he can be one stubborn little man
We try to discipline and reward
But most of the time he gets bored
He plays with his treats as if they were toys
He walks with his head high like one of the boys
Every day with him is a pleasure
Even when he is moaning about the weather.

Sadie

Man's Best Friend

From a young pup to a wise old hound
I'm always glad that you're around
To me you are a real godsend
The one and only man's best friend.

Unconditional love you give
No matter how I choose to live
No questions asked, no reprehend
The loyalty of man's best friend.

You're at my side both day and night
Never letting me out of sight
True companion to the end
For now and always, my best friend.

Bob Harris

Alas

When I was little I had a budgie, but alas it flew away,
Now I'm older and slightly bolder,
I often wonder where it went on a bright sunny day.
Then sometime later my dad bought me a horse,
But I couldn't ride it, we hung laundry on it – of course.
Then he bought a chicken – I thought he was a winner,
But, alas again, he killed it – we ate it one Sunday dinner.
Again he shelled out on a little lamb, but alas it caught a bug,
Now somebody's easing their feet on it – it ended as a rug!
Then he gave me some goldfish – I thought he shouldn't have oughta,
He thought he'd got away with it, 'til the gold came off in the water.
I haven't had much luck with animals; not even the human style,
My wife buggered off and left me; she's been gone for quite a while.

Warren Fraser

To Be A Ferret

Look out world here I come,
I'm an unseen, keen,
Finder of fun.
Don't be fooled by my small size,
I'll trick you once,
Hello! *Surprise!*
I plan my attack,
And lay in wait,
I'll use my sweet little face as bait.
Look at me!
I'm so darn cute!
Bouncing around,
Boing, boing, toot, toot!
You there! Human.
Are these new socks?
Haha! Now they're mine,
We ferrets rock!
Dook, dook, dook, dook, dook, dook,
Weasel power!
Now I'll nibble your ankles,
And lick your toes.
A big long yawn and,
Time for a doze.

Shele Cox

Beautiful Garden Butterfly

Beautiful garden butterfly
You flutter in a garden a secret hideaway,
Enjoying each warm, sunny day,
Spring casts her magic spell,
To bring you colourful flowers
With sweet nectar you love to smell
You flutter in summer's celebration,
Nature lives up to your high expectation,
You flutter among flowers
And leaves in the summer breeze
Where the air feels
So light and airy,
You flutter around like a dainty fairy,
You love living the dream,
You love to smell the garden's
Freshly mown lawn so evergreen,
You're the apple of everyone's eye,
Beautiful garden butterfly.

Joanna Maria John

Our Eli

Our Eli is a rescue cat,
Taken in as a stray,
Nurtured back to health and
Microchipped against further wanderings
Before being put up for adoption.

Obviously loved and well cared for by his
Previous owner, judging by his sweet nature
And soft, luxurious coat,
Which begs the question, what went wrong?
Did they die, or move away,
Or was he put outside in disgrace
Following some feline misdemeanour and,
Thinking he was banished for life,
Wandered off?
We will never know.

I went astray once
Following one telling-off too many,
Which left me feeling unloved and worthless.
I didn't stray far, it's true,
But did wander around in the wilderness of sin,
Searching for meaning to my
Feelings of desperation, inadequacy and failure,
Until I, too, was rescued,
Nurtured back to sanity
And marked with the Seal of Righteousness
By my Heavenly Father
For all time.

Kathy Rawstron

Meadows Of Caramel

I followed her along the path,
Warm,
Skipping soulful bliss,
The ears so finely tuned and poised
To catch the musical garden sound.
In meadows bounce,
Season decanters all around with all paws on ground,
Fallow fields burnt to live once more as fur,
Soft and staving,
And beautiful,
Meanders through maize and wheat,
Yes – a little golden coin on her way,
Searching,
Prolonging,
Biting her way towards the
Core, erupt companionship and nature and harmony in a touch,
Back in my arms once more,
Smooth and subtle as child would be fresh born,
Heaven alive as I set you to safety in this enclosed Elysium,
Free in my keep and a friend to my soul,
Burning flames of light and singing,
Ears pick up to my voice as my eyes flick open to your sight,
Bring me harvest and rejoice,
Rejoice, rejoice,
Old for new and critter as man,
Brother and friend,
Skip on my young one,
Skip on by –
Yet watch me,
As I follow.

Edward Searle

Memories Of A Pet

My cat would always sit, refined.
Moving with a silky tread.
Black fur flashing in my mind.

Social action, disinclined.
Present only to be fed,
My cat would always sit, refined.

Pillowcase with cat-hair lined,
Newspapers only used to shred,
Black fur flashing in my mind.

Spot of sunlight always find,
Any surface used as bed,
My cat would always sit, refined.

Fabric from the chairs unwind
Across unwilling knees she spread.
Black fur flashing in my mind.

Alone, I wish time to rewind.
But my cat is gone and dead.
My cat would always sit, refined,
Black fur flashing in my mind.

Alexander McCall

Buster's Poem

What's that feathered thing behind my bed?
It's small, it's brown, I can't see its head.
It's trying to hide, it's scared to come out.
Nobody scream, nobody shout.
My dad's here to move it out the back door,
There's no need for it to be scared anymore.
I now get a treat for being a good boy,
A walk and a stroke, a play with my toy,
I am tired and happy as I go to bed,
Knowing the bird that I found has now fled.

Adam Crawley

My Feline Friend

My sweet little Lucy is by my side each day
She's always with me every step of the way
Her unconditional love she gives so much of
She's a precious treasure sent from above.

She snuggles up close so I can stroke her fur
Her eyes slowly closing as she starts to purr
She asked for nothing but tender loving care
She just needs to know I will always be there.

Her shining eyes and her grey coat so fine
She is a real beauty, she's my loyal feline.
She brings me much joy by being around
She's a treasure I was lucky to have found.

I can't imagine how empty life would be
Without my friend who means the world to me
With whom I have such an awesome bond
That in just a short time has grown so strong.

Monica Partridge

Madge

Tall and slender body lovely curvy spine
A tiny little button nose you sure are my feline
Little furry boots with little white toes
You pussycats sure know how to pose

Big green eyes a coat of black
A tail so long you sure can whack
I have had you for a long time
My little furry friend everywhere I go

You're always round the bend
Going to the shops I see you duck and dive
I am surprised you made it this long
You must have used nine lives.

Caroline Ferguson

Heaven's Bird

The singing I used to hear every morning,
Still plays in my head so vividly,
The way you always used to spread your wings,
Seemed like light beamed out from every angle.
His wings, blue as the clear sky,
As he flew softly from corner to corner.
His shiny eyes that looked like the stars at night,
Came clear to me that he's unique.
Different to other birds.
The difference was he's my heart,
Part of my heart, you're always in it,
Alive forever.

Sara Gamil. Rahman

Maisie

Maisie is a lovely dog, the breed that 'King Charles' bought,
A cavalier finely bred, an aristocratic sought.
With big brown eyes, that roll around and fur so red and white,
So docile is her nature, she really would not fight.
She fetches balls and titbits while wagging her long tail,
To reward her with a loving stroke will never really fail.

Sitting on her quarters, alert with ears raised,
Looking like a pot dog, the type glossed and glazed.

But Maisie is no ornament
A heart beats there inside.
A friend, a loyal companion
Who gives us so much pride.

Christine Stafford

Fizzy

F izzy is our tortoise, she
I s very fast
Z oom
Z oom she does go
Y ou are fantastic Fizz.

Charlotte Mills (10)

Faithful Friends
(For Tina and Bonny)

Mother and daughter snuggled up in bed
Eating out the same food bowl when it was time to be fed.
My little Jack's always by my side,
Brave and courageous, so full of pride
Running through the park, chasing each other around
Picking up sticks of every bit of ground.
Just wanting lots of cuddles, kisses on your furry heads
Tucked up with your chew sticks and toys in your comfy bed.
It seems like yesterday but you're both no longer here
My heart still feels embedded in a frozen tear.
Of missing you which has been hard to bear
But memories and thoughts will always make me care.
Up in Heaven, healthy and happy now
Free of pain, just lots of sunshine, no more rain.
So goodnight little ones, will see you when I sleep
As tears fall on my pillow as I gently weep.

Irene Burns

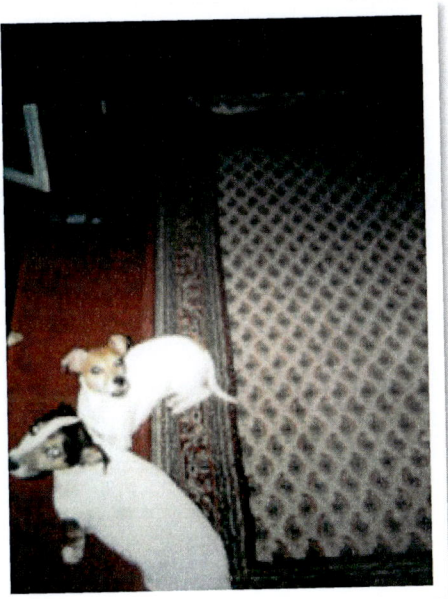

The Cat

The cat that always stares at me,
The cat that always miaows or purrs.
When I'm walking and it sees me
It stops, it freezes, doesn't stir.

When on the other side
It passes both my friends
Just to miaow and gaze into my eyes
Will there come a day when this tradition ends?

It's like we are family
Related in a past life.
Mother and daughter
Mother and son or even husband and wife.

We share something special
Contact of the eyes.
Connection, like we've known each other
Forever, I tell no lies.

The cat is gone
It is not dead
The time has come
For the tradition to end.

I go to school with a new friend
Day after day
And we walk
A different way.

Carmina Masoliver

Crazy Cats

C ats are crazy
R osie liked to cuddle close
A jay the silly kitten jumped in the bin
Z ooming across the floor making us grin
Y ou need to keep the kittens safe

C ats are cool
A ston was a shy kitten
T offee and Fudge were our first foster kittens
S tay in our hearts when they find their forever home.

Daniel Mills (7)

Ben McLean McWoof

I'm a golden lab – a social hound
With a face Lassie would bark for
Soft toys are my favourite gifts
I can carry three in my jaws
And oh – by the way,
I've got polishing pads for paws!

The Canine Club are proud of me
I've got three doggy ASBOs!
On a walk of recent duration I found
And ate a cabbage
Trouble was I rued my prize
It did my digestion ravage!

My first ASBO was for pink Camay
Which I ate and foamed at the mouth
The vet told Louisa, 'Don't you fret
It's a cross to bear for a lab as a pet!'

My latest doggy scoff was a tasty Sheila sock
Which traversed through my tummy's sack
Although she doesn't want it back!

When people call to see my kin
And bring some cakes to eat
I put my face between my paws
And pose engagingly at their feet

I wait my moment carefully –
Their vigilance I will trounce!
I'll claim my cake with a
Joyful woof just before I pounce!

You see I'm like Bruce Forsyth
A swift and deft mover
They won't have to worry about any crumbs
I'm an ace canine Hoover!

Yours woofingly Ben
From the pen of Patsy.

Patsy McLean

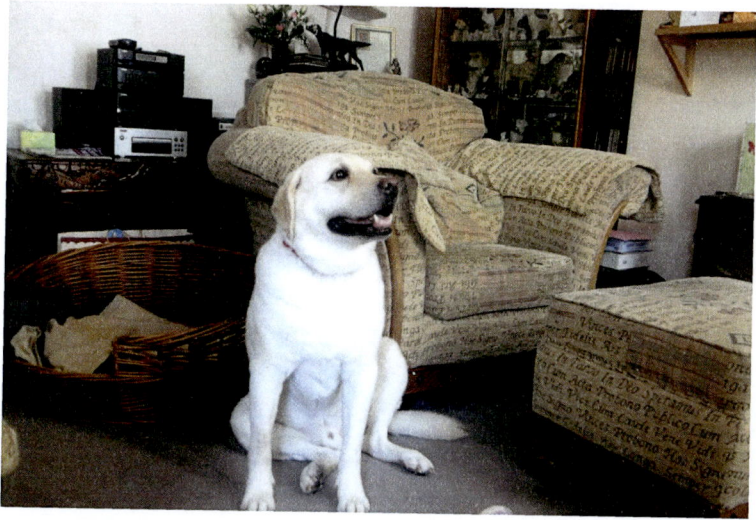

Our Crazy Tortoise

We have a tortoise whose name is Fizz
We call her Fizz the Whiz
She's very fast you see
She darts across the garden
Quicker than you or me
She bangs her shell to say I'm hungry
She bangs to say I'm awake and feeling lively
She's a very nosey tortoise
She likes to say hello
She listens for new voices
Then back in her shell she will go
She loves the smell of pizza
That always wakes her up
She rushes over to greet you
And looks and begs you to share
When you tell her she's not allowed
She sulks and shows you her bum
But when you offer her strawberries
She soon forgets to be glum
She's a very funny tortoise
She has a character of her own
We've had her since she was a baby
And boy, she's really grown
She makes us laugh every day
With her funny little quirks
She's a big part of our family
And we love her in every way.

Carena Mills

A Right Little Charlie

A squirming lump of loveliness
Full grown but immature
Chihuahua crossed with Papillon
A pedigree impure

So tiny yet so powerful
He's wilful, loud and strong
A little thug, a ruffian
Who's never in the wrong

A blatant nosy parker he
The neighbours have no clue
How closely Charlie studies them
In everything they do

For scavenging and snooping
Charlie has a special knack
But any hint of censure
Sends him rolling on his back

A sense of humour's vital
Charlie trembles at a frown
Life's fun – sharp words and bossiness
Pull Charlie's spirits down

To jest and tease is Charlie's way
For everything's a game
He'll scamper round with wagging tail
When called to heel by name

He loves to talk – in squeaks and trills
Of varied note and tone
And answers back instinctively
In language all his own

His bedding strewn across the floor
With toys and nylon bone
He has to be the most untidy
Dog I've ever known

Affectionate and comical
Creative in his play
Enchanting, cheeky, bright, alert
A source of joy each day.

Helen Clarke

Salem

'Sixty pounds?' my mother cried
'You paid as much as that!
It seems an awful lot to pay
Just to buy a cat!'
She didn't understand though
The reason that I did
I thought that it was worth it
To pay our sixty quid.
Your green eyes so appealing
Your fur so soft and black
And when I stroked you
I really loved
The way you stretched your back.
I've brought you home
You've settled in
Salem is your name.
'Twas the thirteenth and a Friday
The very day you came.
And so your name was easy
You look like a witch's cat
So how could I give to you
Any name but that.
As you grew
It was plain to see
How beautiful you are
The mischief in your eyes
Make them twinkle
Like a star.
But you can be so gentle
Body full of grace
And when you want attention
You softly stroke my face.
I know that
I belong to you
Your servant to the end
But you make it very clear to me
You'll always be my friend.
I really love you baby girl
I don't know what I'd do
If something happened
You weren't around
My heart would break
It's true.

So I will make the most of you
Appreciate every day
Until the time comes
Years from now
You have to go away.

Patricia Lee Sheen

Rosie, At Ten And A Half

She playfully stalks the smallest game,
or sits in a cardboard box, like Jack
without the spring; that furry dame
has many a surprise to pack

into the parcel of a day.
An athlete's warm-up stretch invites
a stroke, then fur flows the right way.
Grey-brown markings are muted, slight.

A creamy locket round her neck
tilts left, with no sign of a chain.
It's decorated with a speck
of ginger. She treats with disdain
those plush collars, with tinkly bells,
or gewgaws that the pet-shop sells.

Gillian Fisher

Marley Wolfgang Martin

Marley Wolfgang Martin, handsome in black and white,
Immaculate always, his appearance just right.
When his friends come to visit he really does show off,
He preens and cleans and ends up looking like a toff.
His menu is varied and he always leaves his plate so clean
Favourites include carrots and anything that is green.
Marley leads a contented very simple kind of life,
No grief or worries for him and certainly no strife.
This special young man of stature very small
Marley Wolfgang Martin is the rabbit loved by all.

Linda Martin

Men In Fancy Dress

Such clowns and crowd-pleasers
Posing calmly for the cameras
Neither shy nor reticent
To display their daily lives
Each gesture and posture
Behaviour and expression
Perfectly matched
As they sit side by side
And stare into each other's eyes.

Sleeping, eating, playing
In full view, unafraid
These slow, gentle creatures
Endearing and enduring
Such deliberate actions and attitudes
Oblivious to their keepers' attentions
In these parkland pens

Symbols and souvenirs of their species
Precious panda merchandise
Raising vital funds for breeding research
Daily bamboo diet and long-term preservation
For sale now in the tourist shop

But these cannot be wild creatures
Rescued from their habitat
With heads and hands and feet
Large enough to get into
Their black and white costumes
The right size and shape
For men to live inside
And provide the daily show
For a thousand photographs

The actors, for actors they must be,
Practised in their antics
Always sitting in the right positions
For maximum exposure
This cannot be natural
For them to co-operate so well
The pandas, for pandas they cannot be
Must be but men in fancy dress.

Andy Fawthrop

George

The cat's gone. Black with a white mark
and a hole in one sock, he went out
and never came back.

No trace of him on the two roads.
No black fur, blood-matted, in any gutter.
No track in the woods.

He's disappeared. Utterly.
The red fish relaxes lazily
in the pond, under the lily.

No lapping disturbs or scares.
The slates, roughly positioned around,
still loose, don't ever rock.

Maybe some shed
was investigated, key turned in lock
conscientiously

without noticing
the scrap of fur-trimmed life
furtive in one corner.

Just so, a moment's carelessness
extinguishes a small love, and when you return,
something that mattered is missing.

Carole Robertson

George was well. Many months later he was spotted on the edge of town. He had perhaps
left to get away from a big brother and seek his own fortune elsewhere like
Dick Whittington's cat. He had found another place to call home.

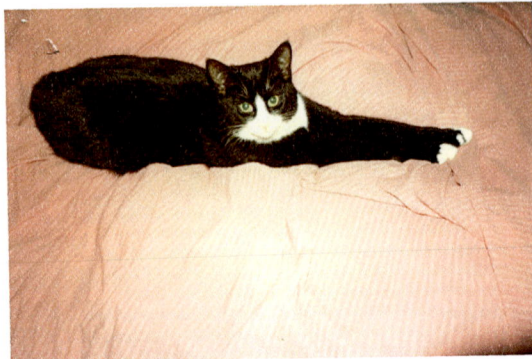

Adapting

Since I was a little kid
Loving animals was all I did
Spending days with cats and dogs
Jumping round with toads and frogs
Horses were always in favour
Riding them I would savour
Have a chatter with a parrot
Tempt a bunny with a carrot
Look at fish under a lake
Excited interest I would take
My love of pets never stopped
Until out my allergies popped
I can't be with fur or feathers
Or anything held back with a tether
But now I've found another way
To keep loving animals every day
I simply adore a Slytherin snake
My friends just say, 'Oh goodness sake!'
They don't know what I see in them
I see another slippery friend
Something to give all my love
But not be allergic to like a dove
Snakes are nothing but the best
Slytherin better than the rest.

Sophie Rawlings

James The Cat

Happiness is sharing everything with James my fluffy black cat
Sharing my bed, my food and the spot where I was sat
I wake up to the sound of his heart-warming purr
I roll over and stroke his soft silky fur
He comes to kiss me with his black soggy nose
I tell him I love him but he already knows
I get up to feed him, it's tuna today
He wolfs it down does my little Bombay
Let's go in the garden and watch the birds fly
It's so peaceful outside just James and I
Indoors we go now as we see April showers
Next it's the brown mouse toy and we play for hours
He chases his shadow all over the room
He stops for a while for a wash and a groom
It's nearly bedtime again for me and my moggy
I could never trade him in for a fish or a doggy
We snuggle again as the lights start to dim
My bed's never empty when it's me and him
I ruffle his ears and say, 'Goodnight James'
What a lovely day spent playing silly games
Now off to sleep for Jamesy and me
We'll do it all again tomorrow just you wait and see!

Amy Rennocks

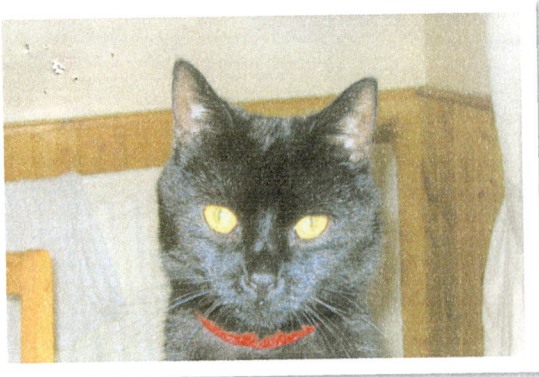

My Four-Legged Friend

There are times in life when it's hard to see
Who in my life actually cares about me.
I obviously have family and friends that care
But they're busy too and aren't always there.
However there is one character, there till the end
Who comes in the form of my four-legged friend.
The strength of a great giant, if only she knew
The array of troubles she has helped me through.
Always provides a nuzzle when times are rough
And an encouraging bark when things get too tough.
She's playful and boisterous, always up for fun
Then searches for a cuddle when playtime is done.
No, she's not a real person, she doesn't talk back
But she pulls me through everyone else being slack.
Clumsy as a fool yet somehow delicate, like a dove,
She offers a guarantee to always be full of love.
That's how I know there's someone who'll be there till the end
And she comes in the form of Emmy, my four-legged friend.

Charlotte Barnes

Surrogate Dad

A cosy place
to lay my head,
Loving owners,
and a nice warm bed.
I am top dog,
and the feeling's good,
No one to beg
or steal my food.

I've been single
All my life,
and never wanted
Pups or wife.
My peace and quiet
is dear to me,
The house is mine
to do as I please.

But then!
the tragic day arrives,
My peace destroyed
by whinging cries.
The family smile
but I'm not glad,
They have a pup,
Oh! This is bad.

It runs to me
with real delight,
Then mounts my back,
Now! that's a fright.
It bites my ear
and sniffs my bum,
Then snuggles up
like he's my chum!

My master fawns
With affectionate oohs,
But the pup gets excited,
and squats down and poos.
Oh! That is gross,
Has he no shame?
I don't even know
the stinker's name.

I look to the Boss,
For support and advice.
But he just said,
'Pup, you're so nice,
get in your bed,
See if it suits.
And Kipper be nice
To your new friend Boots.'

Be nice, I think,
You must be mad.
I'm much too young
To be a dad.
But in the end
the silly pup wins,
My serenity destroyed,
and Bedlam begins.

Jeanette Bramald

A Lovable Rascal

Each day is a game of chase and fun
From the minute his eyes open
He has you on the run
Life was fairly orderly

There was a familiar routine
Not anymore since Archie came on the scene
What he loves best of all
Is for you to chase him

Whilst on the run he'll grab anything he can
While you stand there hovering
Pondering your next move
He cheekily juggles his ill gotten gains high in the air
Everything getting pierced, battered and bruised

He's very sociable and friendly loves to go for a walk
Boisterous and bouncy
The other dogs can't wait to get out of his way
It doesn't seem to bother him
He'll find another way around it

Patiently behind the fence he'll sit
All time to the last minute to wait
For neighbours, people who happen to pass by
Up pops his head for them to stop, tickle or pat him
That really makes his day.

Angela Wells

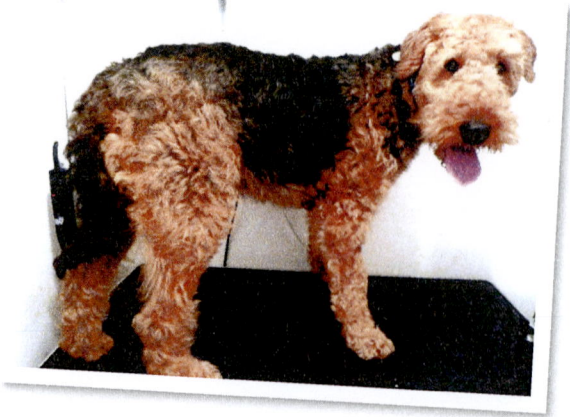

The Boss

Robin.
On the bird table.
On the patio chair.

Letting me know he is waiting
To be fed
Now.

For him
The now is all
There is.

For me
The now is a new adventure
To take.

He is the boss
The master
Who knows.

I am the novice
The initiate
Who trusts.

Together
We give each other
Everything.

William Weavings

Dumbo Jet

A dog wandered into my sister's school playground,
She found no one to claim him though she asked all around.
No missing dog reported to the police, so in the end
He came home with us and became our loyal friend.

He raced madly round, had huge ears and was black as night,
So calling him Dumbo Jet seemed to fit him just right.
Though he guarded us all, for his owner he chose me
And after our morning walk, enjoyed buttered toast and tea.

He never barked at the postman or doorbell though his hackles rose up
So we guessed he'd been punished, for barking, as a pup.
But when my brother-in-law tickled me, made me squeal and fall back,
Surprisingly he barked at John, then growled, ready to attack.

At first he stole food and chewed everything in sight,
Slippers, socks, even two five pound notes tasted right!
For thirteen happy years Dumb Jet was our true and faithful friend
And was so sadly missed when old age overtook him in the end.

Eileen Ballance

The Elephant Who Forgot

The elephant who forgot
was not
a happy beast.
The others teased him until his big grey ears were red.
('Beneath the skin they're red,'
he said.) But though his memory was bad
that was no reason for him to be sad
or even flush a tiny blush of shame,
for every elephantine day
is just the same,
and happiness happens in the same and uneventful way
as it did yesterday
and yesterdays yesterday.
So everything our elephant forgot
will happen just the same again. A lot.

Fred Brown

Scaredy Cat

I own a tabby cat,
he's so big, round and fat.
But there is just one thing,
this cat is scared of everything.
One day by chance he met a mouse,
in fright, he puffed up like a house.
Cat leapt quickly onto the chair,
whilst the mouse just sits down there.
He shivered, quivered and shook,
wore a pale distraught look.
Oh goodness, what an affray,
his stripes turned a very pale grey.
Then from outside came a loud clump,
shot three foot in the air, like a chump.
While the mouse relaxed eating chocolate,
I'm afraid our cat just bottled it.
Cat shot through the door like a rocket,
the frightened mouse, leapt into my pocket.
Now it's me that's up on the chair,
throwing my jacket high into the air.
The last time I saw this mouse,
he was quickly leaving our house.
But our cat won't come back in,
stays shivering behind the dustbin.
Are we a couple of mouse nervous sprats
or maybe a couple of scaredy cats?

Josephine Smith

George The Blind Rottweiler

George the Rottweiler pup,
was born blind.
He didn't know any different,
so he did not really mind.

Shipped over from Ireland
feeling lost and alone.
Waiting for someone to rescue him,
from the dog home.

Then one day,
someone did come,
to take him home
and to be his mum.

His eyes were gone,
they would never mend.
But his mum had other dogs,
who would be his friend.

George would bang into things
and get in a muddle.
But he was always picked up,
and given a cuddle.

Taken for walks
and to be free.
For George there is
no better place to be.

Kevin Crookes

The Girls

Now we've retired we could get a pet
What to get we don't know yet
A dog, a cat, it all depends
No, we know we'll get some hens

We set to work with wire and wood
A shed with a run, now that looks good
What breed would suit our garden by the sea
Black and white, Light Sussex look good to me

At the farm we decide to buy three, no more
But we can't leave that one on its own
So we end up with four

Straight away they take to their new home
During the day the whole garden to roam
They enjoy themselves all day
At night we shut them away

But in the morning they are out at dawn
Trouble is they have ruined the lawn
But it's alright because of the excellent eggs they lay
At the moment we are getting four a day

Breakfast with eggs so fresh, nest box to pan
We have two each if we can
Excess eggs are given to neighbours and friends
Aggie, Rosie, May and Flo are our garden hens.

Ray Wilson

Boxer-Dog Lil

It's almost obscene to put a dog in a dress,
then I catch you boxer-dog Lil, stretched out on my bed,
with your fur a brindled mix of black and tan,
in dog sleep, sparrow legs warm from sheets
that are supposed to be mine. I do not want the hot reek
of your dog skin on my bed.

You have been delinquent and shy.
You drank my wine and got pregnant that time.
Boxer-dog Lil, your dark face a black mask,
how you shout at those who come to our door.
Though your soft side appears at night,
when you round us to check we are safe.

And you do still have velvet ears,
which you've had from being a suckling pup
and I should have seen that being the boss was tough on you
and that by now, no longer pulled from teats to tail by children,
your crumpled face, with scattering of grey
has earned the right to nuzzle for a softer place.

So I watch, as both your eye-lids flicker
over small squinty eyes, your nose twitches a bit, wet black,
and your rib cage rises and falls
as you blow breath through those,
almost rudely kissable lips.

Georgina Wilson

For Paddington

You were there when I needed,
Always by my side,
A love that will last a lifetime,
A pain I cannot hide.

Yet not too long I've known you,
But enough to know my love is true
And never did I question
The love I had for you.

There are people out there I blame for this,
All those if buts and maybes,
But none of those will bring you back
My darling little baby.

I hope you can forgive me
Because I only blame myself.
You looked so sad and helpless,
I couldn't nurse you back to health.

I loved you little Paddington
So lovely and talented you were.
I'm so sorry for the pain you felt
But I know you're not too far.

Amelia-Georgia Clarke

Little Blackbird

Little blackbird, coarse and twisted
Wings unformed, screech horrific
Weak and motherless, boxed and fed
Out of nest, to live on bread

Perched on my finger, batteries included
Wings flap with fun, so hurry home
Such joy awaits at end of day
A morsel of cabbage, fate delayed

Warm winds of summer, strong rays of sun
Garden's green, flowers life
Soon he'll fly and be his own
Sail the breeze, then come home

'Worms,' said Dad, 'From his mother's breast!'
An innocent child, laid to rest
A flapping soul, I'll never forget
With bread and tears, he lies there dead

Little blackbird, coarse and twisted
I love you so, my heart's blistered.

Coleman King

Father Tree

The moisture of life sucked through our roots so you may grow tall
With branches entwining and intermingling amongst the leaves
You kill other life so you may exist, survive and thrive
Birds nestle in the summit of your glory in nests of twig and mud.
Squirrels run along your vast spreading magnificence
Popping shells of nuts as they scamper and twitch.
Children climb up you as a sense of adventure
They treat you like a climbing frame
Fall in your fall and graze their knees
Oh father tree why don't you walk tall for hundreds of years
In the dense forests of the world?

Matthew Lee

A Sense Of Humour?

Dogs and horses, cats and hamsters,
I have had them all.
Yet I've never kept a tiger, never bathed an elephant
or looped a snake into a coil.

So many characters
I recall,
from a horse who switched the light on when I left his stall,
to a dog who opened sideboard drawers so he could reach his ball.

And a little cat who teased the next-door moggy,
knowing he would chase.
But she also knew her cat-flap was too small
for him to squeeze inside the hall.

Their antics pleased me through their lives
I'm sure they saw the humour,
repeating tricks which caused a fuss,
so pleasing them as well as us.

June Sharp

Ode To Coco

We lie locked together,
trading warmth a circle of companionship and comfort
in the still, quiet moments of evening.

Breathing in and out in unity, a melody
of togetherness, the rise and fall ties us
in ways that daytime motion could never do.

We touch, the briefest of connections,
soft fingertips, an errant toe or perhaps
the gentlest of nibbles, entirely justified.

And then, just when I am lulled almost to sleep
by our velvet twinning, you emit a tiny, almost dainty
kitten fart and I push you onto the floor.

Claire Jones

135

Feline

So delicate and rare am I
I sleep beneath the stairs do I
Adored by all who pass me by
Most precious apple of their eye!
This form so slender and divine
My graceful head, such perfect line
No other shall compare with mine!
I doubt that ever on this Earth
Shall thee behold such splendid worth.
My eyes outshine your precious pearls
My equal? Please forgive yourselves!
You know not what you say
I rise above your lowly souls
Amusing as you are
I must maintain the status quo
And know you find it hard!
Your eagerness to please me
Shall soon have its reward!
Now leave me be upon your chair
In dappled sunshine's loving care,
Sweet catnap dreams their secrets share,
My heart's desire awaits me there
Enchanted streams of double cream,
My favourite toys upon the trees
Are mice in search of leaves of cheese?
No dogs allowed, nor circus fleas,
And fur balls nevermore shall be!
The bringers of reality,
These cruel destroyers of my sleep
I share with you, how kind of me!
I truly am a wondrous creature
My every inch is my best feature!
Superior and worldly wise
Exquisite coat, and greenest eyes,
Oh how I must light up your lives!
You're precious treasured proud feline!

Rob Cunningham-Caskie

Wolves

The snow is white
The moon trembles, full
With words so wild
They utter themselves

Night dancers, grey hunters
Lupi. Too many vowels
To twist a tongue around

Our red blooded mouths
Swashing with sound.

Drag marks left
Lead to the woods
The terrified moon, full
The snow is white.

Charles Baylis

My Crazy Cats

Totts came to us all in tats,
He's the newest of our cats.
Torta's always laid by the fire,
She must think it's time she should retire.
Twinkle looks like a skunk,
You would sometimes think she was a punk.
She's so fluffy but also toughie
Then there's our Lucky, who is very black
And always whacking the other cat's back.
Then there's our Tigger, who's a real scaredy cat
Who only comes out at night just like the bats.
This is why I call them all my crazy cats.

Lisa Beaumont

Suhlia Al Hayat (Lizard Life)

Claws on all fours the mini spike king
On a cricket match with a toothful grin
The desert hunter the secret keeper
The dark hardback bedroom leaper
The shoulder creeper away from harm
Deceiving with his looks but filled with charm
The intellect rises off the heat mat
With legs that perform like an acrobat
Suspicion rises within his eyes
The protector of his land vivarium sized
The home heat bather, woodchip scraper
Boisterous moth chaser, mini love maker
The scaly rock climber livestock finder
The green leave consumer of appetisers
The active fartlek fearless arm waver
The head bopping brave heart stone creeper
The bearded roughneck pogona vitticep
Sensor chaser with sound check
The receptive non simplistic expressionistic
Naturalistic socialist
Filling the palm of my Egyptian hand
From the sand of the habitat that greets salaam
A real fascination jungle attraction
With the egg that hatched in reptile action
The fierce face of memory caption
That bad boy buddy that's my beard dragon.

Nadia Fahmy

I Love Horses

H orses can run very fast
O ver jumps, who is last?
R iding is my favourite thing it makes me want to sing.
S tirrups are where you put your feet.
E ating Polos is their favourite treat.
S tables are where they like to sleep.

Jasmin Young

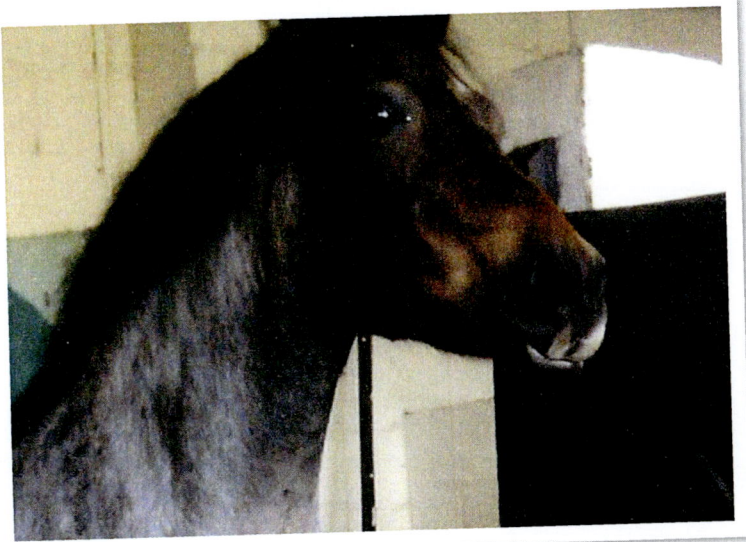

Lycosa Tarantula
(For Rachel Shelley)

I move very slowly
And make no sound –
My legs are eight
My body is round.
I'm large as a saucer
My eyes are bright –
My fur's soft and silky
I'll give you a fright!

But don't be scared
My sting's been removed –
We could be good friends
That I have proved.
I'll climb on your palm
And rest for a while –
And if you stay calm
Why – I'll give you a smile!

Delia Marheineke

Felis Catus

Cat Are Tigers Sherkhans
Agile Tabbies Super Cool
Tinker Sadie Cobalt Amber
Stalking Carnivorous Attacking Terror

Cobalt Ate The Sparrow
Amber Tasted Ambrosia Cream
Tinker Stretched Catnapped away
Sadie Toyed Sat Contented

Cobalt Amber Tinker Sadie
Admired The Silver Cockatoo
Taunted, Sadly Caged Above
Sadie Cased A Turtledove.

David M Walford

The One-Armed Bandit

Not a gambler
I went into the betting shop nonetheless.
Surveyed the temptations
mewing vying for my investment.

Tiny tails quivered like quill pens
dipped in ink whiskers twitched noses
pressed to cages weighing up my gullibility –
here's a right mug.

Drawn ot one cappuccino and cream
ball of fluff, back turned to the world,
scowled privately in disgust at his cell mates
prostituting themselves in the hope of a decent home.

One sunflower-yellow eye opened a crack
for evil eye-to-scared stiff eye contact.
Bugger off. Leave me alone.
I left with my winnings!

Eighteen years living in a war zone –
He tolerated the finest food,
silk pillows, pride of place by the fire
personal grooming and prawns every week.

Eighteen years living in occupied territory –
his.
Front forepaw now lame,
his disdain for us is fever pitch
like an old human, fully aware but
powerless, immobile.

Independence gone – fed at one end,
wiped out at the other.
Attitude still the same –
looks down at us as he looks up –
(how does he do that?)
As though we are to blame.

He has given up, I think, and so have we.
There is no hope after
eighteen years addiction
to the one armed bandit.

Sharon Jane Lansbury

Pippin

I had a dog that was just grand, proper buffalo
of a friend. Slyvie would laugh as it went for
high fives in the garden, while the kettle boiled.

She'd totter along following the smell of ham
on the wind, quickly spin and sit as she forgets
why she totters – dog and owner alike.

When she got ill no one panicked, no spring chicken
our Pip. Andy next door reckoned it was done
'No point forking out cash, let it go! Jesus Christ.'

She'd never high-five Andy, six foot sceptic.
A mechanic. Bexhill, heart of iron and stone soul.
'Don't see men like that mourn for anything'

Sylvie says. But when pip died, any heart,
any mechanic would stop and understand
why Sylvie and I cried, at her last totter.

Natalie Rogers

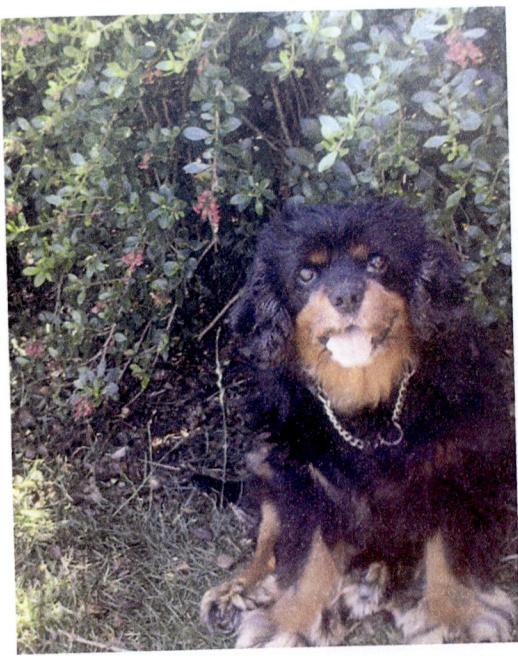

A Great Top-Dog

Peggy was very much part of my family who owned the road, she would bark anybody away,
patrolling the gate and paths.
She was a lovely beautiful retriever cross collie,
with her colourful golden coat, with hair falling out in handfuls.

She would follow me to school and somehow return home, and would get into mischief,
but have that innocent face.
My brothers and I, would tease her, but never bit us,
she loved walks and I miss her pricked up ears as she heard any word.

She enjoyed her food, especially Christmas chocolates 'Good Boys' and was very jealous,
always loved the attention.
Her wagging tail I can still see, chasing cats away,
and had great pleasure in jumping the wall or hiding under the tree.

She sadly died at the great age of 13 on 17th May 1989,
that final sad day ended in a wonderful memorable funeral.
She was my father's faithful lady and she knew this,
a great reliable companion and loyal friend in my young days.

Adrian Bullard

My Loving Friend

I miss the little black shadow called Sweetie
Who was taken away from me.
She was always there beside me
Or sitting on my lap.

She came a young frightened feral cat
Who was in kitten at the time.
So hungry and thirsty
For what she was about to do.

Three kittens found, so we fed her
Until the kittens were nearly full grown.
Two kittens were homed together
We kept the small black one who looked like Mum.

The kitten we kept was the smallest
So we called her Tween of course.
And though always a little aloof
She knew that she belonged to us.

Sweetie and Tween played and slept together
Less than a year in age apart.
Both lithe and slim and colour black,
We had such a job to tell them apart.

Both spayed and had a passport
So off to the south of France to live.
They would follow us for miles,
Across our fields and through our woods.

At the end of a lane to nowhere
Was a haven to us all.
In the heat of summer they'd find shade
Or in front of a log burner, in winter time.

On returning home one night, no Sweetie did we find
But we found, Tween all fast asleep.
I called Sweetie for over an hour,
Though didn't hear her greeting call, miaow.

I donned a coat and grabbed a torch
And trekked our fields and woods at length.
I found her dead, cold and wet
On the side of our quiet lane.

As I held her close to warm her,
I buried my face into her fur.
Through the tears I softly spoke her name
In the hope to awake her from her sleep.

But my little black shadowy furry friend
Would follow me no more.
But her memory it will stay with me
Until the day I die.

My little black loving furry friend
The one that I called sweetie.
I missed you then and I miss you now
And so for evermore, sleep tight.

Norman Armfield

The Gorilla And The Dog

Two good friends
Whose love transcends
The gap twixt type and breed
They together play
Each every day
And a happy life they lead

An unlikely pair
The love they to share
This life they have together
Come rain or shine
They're always fine
That's how they'll stay forever

These lessons are for learning
Their benefits for earning
But man is blind to could see
Once we could in times gone past
But with modern man it did not to last
Take heed at what could be.

Ray Ryan

Little Whippy

'It's just that coming into this world isn't easy for a child
Let alone for pets and a sweet tiny puppy
'Cause who knows how long the love will last for little Whippy.'

Was she a vet or some ruthless midwife?
That shook Whippy to check for signs of life
When all she need do was feel for a pulse
'Oh dear, yes, it's very much alert and with us
Even though it looks like it's not alive
And been pulled through a hedge backwards.'

'Hanna's doggy has gone some lovely sweep puppies
Can I have one for my birthday?
Please Mummy let me have a little Whippy?'

Little Whippy, all wet and slippy
With ears all droopy and light as feathers
As the faintest of murmurs are present,
And just because those eyes remain closed
Don't mean the little creature is lost
Because all she needs is her mother's love.

'Hanna is so lucky she has two dogs, a cat and sister,
I'm fed up with that boring hamster and it stinks!
Oh please Mummy don't be horrible, just let me have a little Whippy.'

The light grey one is the darling of the litter
So delicate, fluffy, cute and sure is a girl.
It won't be long before she's getting into trouble!
And it almost looks like she's smiling
As she's all snuggled up and warm
With her two brothers and sister fast asleep

'A doggy is for always not just your birthday darling
And I can see you soon getting bored with it
Wanting to play with your friends and not taking out little Whippy.'

Thomas McDougall

Bright Eyes

You were always there to welcome me, if I came to call
and I'd reach out to touch you, as you sat there in the hall.
Happiness was yours; just watching the children play
just like sleeping and eating, an important part of your day.

When I sat in the chair, you'd climb upon my knee
and with those bright eyes of yours, turn to look at me.
After a while you'd climb back down, heading for the door
going outside into the night to explore a little more.

You were always happy, when I took you in my arms
I could never help falling, for all your little charms
and wherever I go in my life and whatever I may do.
I'll never meet another cat more beautiful than you.

Tim Kitchen

My Welsh Corgi Dog

You are my best friend in all the world
you can't wag your tail
but that never fails to amuse me.

Pommy botton you have big ears too
bigger than your legs
and you're upside down when you have to beg.
But that only makes me laugh!
You are a dwarf dog
when you sleep you sleep like a log.
Snoring all the time louder and proud.
The very truth of your honest love keeps me faithful to you.
Your love of walkies is so true.
You are my great love and friend till the very end.
It is a true marriage.

Elizabeth Phillips-Scott

Homing Birds

Pigeons are extraordinary contraptions
To climate conditions they make adaptions.
Do they have a magnetic force?
That keeps them accurate in their course.

Mealy, pied, chequered, blue
White, black and brown too.
East, west, north, south
Throughout the air or river mouth.

Navigating ways to their own loft
Returning to their foundation
Sometimes slowly, frequently fast
What a wonderful creation.

Is it the training, the brain or the weight?
That makes the fancier's hobby so great
Or is it the fact that they fly from above
To descend and show their owners love.

Yvonne Baker

My Canine Partner

While I'm just an ordinary person
although I have a disability,
Juneau's trained to be one in a million,
assisting, supporting, inspiring me.

Juneau helps me participate fully
in the mainstream business of living,
people would rather get to know me
instead of looking away or staring.

Juneau is my trusty canine partner,
together we tackle life's ups and downs,
we make a team like you'll find no other
on slopes where once only mountains.

Far more than assistant or friend to me,
Juneau helps make my dreams reality.

Roger N Taber
(For Sheila)

Nursery Knitting Croc
(Inspired by Esmerelda)

She cries in silence as she goes about her daily task
To hide the hurt within and hope no one asks.
For she's a nursery knitting croc,
She spends her days knitting for the new kids on the block.

She works hard and hardly ever plays,
This inevitably, leads to endless days.
The hurt that lies within?
She longs for her own kith and kin.
Ironic and a cruel twist of fate
As she feels unloved, it's all too late.

But these crocodile tears are about to stop,
For look, there's a new handsome croc on the block.
Wow, this should put her fears to rest,
For he is a cut above, the best!

He schmoozes and woos her and well they're in love.
The tears are no more and gone are the endless days.
Things have changed in so many ways.
No sadness now, laughter a lighter mood
As she experiences crocodile tears from her own brood.

Donna Giblin

New House, New Home

Wizard decided he needs a new home
With a flatter garden in which to play
Where birds and cats and squirrels may come
(And mice) and so be chased all day.

And so the hunt began to find him a home
With the usual comforts to call his own
With fences sound so he cannot roam
And net door's guinea pig is left alone.

The very place at last was found
With grassy lawn and dig-able ground
And hiding place for cherished bones
Saved for him by Butcher Jones.

It's not too far to walk to school
Which his owners think is cool
But postmen get an awful fright
If they deliver mail late at night.

But when it gets dark he must not bark
Then he's time to say his prayers
Of God he surely then will ask
'When will they let me go upstairs?'

Jo Allen

Our Type Of Cat

He found our house
In the middle of the night.
He is a pongy, mangy
scruffy type of cat.

He ate all the food
and drank all the milk.
He is a seedy, greedy
wild type of cat.

He comes back every night
but never in the day.
He is a reclusive, illusive
ungrateful type of cat.

He came one dinnertime
with his ear bitten off.
He is a biting, fighting
rough type of cat.

He was taken to the vet
for repair and pills.
He is a hitting, spitting
sulking type of cat.

He'll never be tamed
and will always be free.
He is a wheeler, dealer
spivey type of cat.

He occasionally purrs
when we tickle his chin.
He is a loner, roamer
but he's our type of cat.

Judy Berrow

Flight Of The Red Kite

Centuries ago, bird of prey
the kite
chestnut red, head pale grey
patches white
a predator of skies
in full flight
subdued by traction
lives by predation.

Exterminated in most regions
the kite
hunted for its verminous threat
in flight
fork tailed, with two foot
wing span
not large, aggressive
but how impressive.

One breeding female remained
the kite
incubating in oak trees day
and night
March to April they feed
the young
hunt or preen, eggs will hatch
handing kites a purple patch.

Alex Sarich

Animal Antics

Have you ever wondered what animals think,
At times they mess about.
How they know when to clown around,
When you're feeling slightly down.
Some of them like to mimic and copy what humans do.
Some like to try to do acrobatics thinking they can fly.
Some think they're jugglers,
And try to balance their food bowls in their mouths.
Some think ice skating is chasing one's tail round and round.
These are some of the animal antics.

Gemma Darling

Triggs

His name was Triggs
he was my friend.
With muddy paws and shaggy coat
he'd often drive me round the bend!

Those soulful eyes melted my heart
with bonds of faithfulness and love.
We trudged the highways of our life
for we were never far apart.

Sixteen years of joy and laughs
came to an end one summer day.
When pain had come too much to bear
we lay together on the grass.

The sun shone down on faithful Triggs,
sorrow hard to keep at bay.
Our vet administered relief
and peacefully Triggs slipped away.

I mourn his passing – wouldn't you?
So many happy doggy years
And hoping in my dreaming time
we'll meet again in yonder blue.

Philip Woodford

Cranefiles

Minouchki's chasing craneflies,
of which we have a spate.
Harmless fluttering beasties
litter the verandah
as the demon cat stalks,
leaps and pounces,
feasts on this hors d'oeuvre.
Tiring quickly of this game
of minuscule reward
he miaows for entry,
asks for food,
sits beside the window
making feints at flies outside.

Vivienne Blake

Fat Little Mouse

The little mouse scampers, he weaves here and there
looking to find something and sniffing the air.
A scratch and a wash, then waits for a while,
though he's travelled a short distance to him it's a mile.
His tummy is hungry, his throat is so dry,
but he keeps on going he must or he could die.
He needs some food, he is desperate now
and he begins to get worried seeing the hawk in the sky.

He pops in a hole, one familiar to him
and he remembers a stash he stored there from a bin.
He hurries along the tunnels so dark
but he knows his way so he jumps like a lark.

He arrives at the place, where he stored his food
and his eyes they light up like a greedy fool.
He's been a bit greedy, not left much food at all
but he feels happy and he starts to yawn.
Time for a nap because he feels so fat
but he's now warm and happy, what could be better than that.

Julie Gibbon

Cuddles For You Baby Blue

Creature gentle and so kind,
you shall have a known mind.
Little heart beats unbeaten,
with my cuddles I hope to sweeten.

Phoebe Luckham

Ozzy

He grew with my love like a large English rose
With the thorns of survival equipped for his foes
He learned through experience that life was a test
He knew in his soul that with love he was blessed

The spring of his step, the bounce in his eyes
His clear body language with no lies to disguise
The shine on his velvety dark coat, the white lightning bolt on his chest
Our time spent together flowered with zest

The gentle way he thoroughly sniffs every tree
The way he is always trying to be beside me
The way he softly rests his head on my knee
The way his ears lift and his tail wags when he finds me

The silly expression on his face when we play
The way he sits impatiently when I tell him to stay

The way he jumps up and licks my face when I weep
The strange bits of chewed up toys that he keeps
When I am angry, the way that he sneaks
The way he curls up and purrs like a cat when he sleeps

The way he always has to kiss puppies and kids
The way he always has to sniff dustbin lids

I am partially deaf so he is my ears when I can't hear
When I am feeling scared he always shares my fear
So physically strong, yet his placidity endears
Together so far for over 9 years

The way he jumps over and never walks through the puddle
The way he warms up like an electric blanket when we cuddle

The way he never gives up shows the strength of his will
When he is excited, the way he just can't sit still
The way he comes to me if he is hurt or is ill
Lets me know that he knows just how I feel

He is a bull terrier rooted with instincts to lead him along
With the love in his heart keeping him strong

He knew what he wanted and where to belong
He knew to protect me from all that was wrong

He knew from his pain that love would save him
He knew from me because it was love that I gave him.

Sarah Robertson

Animal Antics

Blaze my dog is a bundle of joy,
She loves to roll while chewing her toy.
She chose me when I needed a friend,
As my husband's life had come to an end.
She was in a litter, a bundle of four
A spotted Springer for whom I adore.
She's the runt, the smallest of all,
Could not make her out while curled in a ball.
She looked and chose me, something she would sense
Ever since then our love is intense.
She loves the sea and loves the sand
But pull her in deep, she scours to land.
She runs around all over the park
But a bit of a coward when it comes to the dark.
I take her for walks when the day disappeared
She has a quick wee, the dark she feared.
She sits on the ground, all stubborn with a groan,
The only way to go now is turn around and back home.
During the day she just can't wait
To pull me along till I get to park gate.
She rolls on her back when the dog walkers around
So they play with her belly, when she's on the ground.
When my phone rings and I move my cup
To be able to answer and put the cushion straight up.
For if the cushion's down, I know it's only time
For my soft chair, is now hers not mine.
My chair becomes a target, while she pretends to sleep
For her chance to get on and make a small leap.
Once she's got on, there's a bit of a grin
As when I get it back, a puddle I'll sit in.
Yes, it's her age, when incontinence hits,
I now buy her own knickers, that snugly fit.
Those seal-like eyes, so big and so sad, I can't tell her off, as I end up sad.
Now she's years older and not as fast,
Every day things become a hard task.
A few more years, hopefully there will be
For us to enjoy each other's company.
I dread the day when we do part
Will hit me hard right in my heart.

Judith Stuart-William

Tibbs And Adolphus

T enaciously your nose twitched
I nstinctively you stared at the piano where a
B owl was delicately perched
B ig eyes stared from it
S kilfully you manoeuvred your way around the ivories

A pproaching with malice aforethought
N ow was the time to commit the
D astardly crime

A rching your back you sprang, sheer
D evilment in your eyes,
O ut you were to catch your
L ong longed for
P rey, but Thomas became the
H ero of the day — he caught the
U nsuspecting fish in his hands —
S cared you slunk away.

Patricia J Tausz

The Dogged Angel

Disengaged from society, why?
Man's best friend
She won't dislike, hate, reject or betray me,
Only love me to the bitter end
As I recoil from the splintered
Spine of human natures dark
In my blackest hour,
The light shines through her echo-laden bark
The die-hard loyalty, the effervescent energy,
It all knows no bounds
When my spirit breaks
She turns and hunts me down like a bloodhound
The tenacious terrier qualities burn bright
As she seeks to console me
In a time when a fractured, frenetic Britain screams loud
She doesn't even know what she does
But her love and affection lift the darkest of clouds.

Chris Botragyi

Animal Antics

When stressful times enfold me,
and my troubles just seem to soar
Just when I've had enough of this
and I just cannot take no more.
In runs my trusted loving friend,
her purrs echoing round the room
And as her nuzzling nose and stinging claws,
slowly dissipate my gloom.
I look into her gorgeous eyes,
intently searching into mine
And I slowly feel this unconditional love
make my sombre mood decline.
As she wraps around my aching frame,
intently nuzzling at my neck
Miaowing discontentment,
jagged tongue gives me a peck.
Her yearning for my soothing hand
to stoke her furry mane
All she wants is a show of my love
which I lovingly maintain.
As I caress her favourite places,
especially behind her ear
She stretches out her languishing frame,
her contentment very clear.
This simple interaction, this truly devoted act
Hits me like a thunderbolt as her love makes its impact.
I'm smiling now, relaxed and content,
all my worries dissipate
As we melt into a timeless void,
in which we both participate.
Time passes like a soundless wind
as we interact and play
An hour of this joyous emotion
and I'm ready for another day.

James Howden

Fizzy

'It's your house, so get a cat!'
But my son wanted a dog.
'When he gets home, he'll love it!'
Or wish instead he had a frog . . .

The kitten was quite beautiful, though,
With a mischievous trait in her prance.
Her black, shiny coat and perfect paws
Was bound to make my son dance.

For sure, the child took a liking
To the young and playful cat.
'She's skitty, a bit witty and quite fizzy!'
And she got her name like that!

A bed was duly made her,
Though she preferred on the chair.
Lounge curtains were stored in the attic,
With window blinds left bare.

The kitten grew in size and skill
And showed such a graceful gait.
Her inquisitiveness and naughtiness
Are still key traits to date.

Fond memories are shared with Fizzy,
Who we have grown to love.
She caresses our feet under the table.
On the chair, we stroke her from above.

Marilyn Bah

Harold The Hare

No bigger than a tiny mouse,
Harold was brought to live in our house.
He was born on a busy airfield,
his mother killed, he needed a shield.
My RAF husband brought him, to me,
to be fed and nurtured till he could go free.
I borrowed our daughter's doll's bottle for milk,
fed him every few hours, made him a nest of silk.
Our four small children all wanted to help,
between us we kept Harold safe on a shelf.
He grew quite rapidly, safe and warm,
protected from any possible harm.
Soon he was running all over our house,
no longer as vulnerable as a mouse.
He quickly became one of the family group
but had access to the garden, wasn't confined to a coop.
At any time he could've gone,
to keep him confined you'd be selfish and wrong.
Harold lived with us for just two years
till one day he went and left us in tears.
But sometimes we saw him out in a field,
he was happily living his life unconcealed.
We never stayed long in any one place,
it was as if Harold knew he had to make his own pace.
Then one day he was just over the fence
with a female beside him looking rather tense!
That was the last time I saw that adorable hare,
he obviously found a friend to share
his life. I think about him wishing him well,
and feel privileged to have helped him for a short spell.
It also taught our children to care
great to know that a love of animals, we all share.

E Eagle

Nibo!

My faithful friend
Who'll be with me until the end.
She never leaves me alone
She's never far behind
Where I roam.
She's loving and funny
Plays around the house
With her toys,
When she wants
Something from you
You can hear her cry.

Her ears go up
When you talk to her and say,
'Nibo, what do you want for your dinner today?'
She goes to the cupboard
When she wants a biscuit
She soon lets you know
If you have forgotten her
And missed it.
Her health's not too good now
She's coming 18
She still jumps around
And likes to know where you have been.
She's nosy and funny
And inquisitive too.
She brings so much pleasure
Watching her play with her toys
Her ears go up when you make a noise
She's always playing
And jumping to and fro
Couldn't imagine
Life on my own now
Without my faithful
Nibo.

Mary Woolvin

Our Friend Bailey

We hear that morning groan
Coming from the dog,
Sounding like an old man
Croaking like a frog,
He struggles with the next step
Cos he's too old to jog.

Next we hear the crunching
As through her food she chomps
Then lapping her water
To wash down any lumps.

Dear old Bailey
We all love her loads
Tiptoeing through the house
Then curling up in repose
At the foot of Francesca's bed
As through the night they doze.

Elizabeth Adams

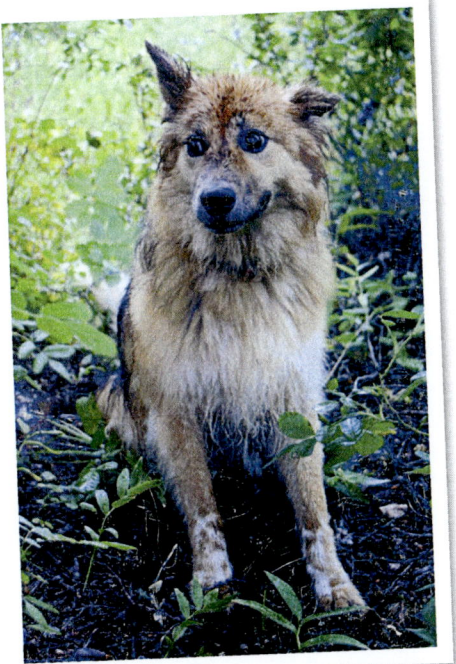

Our Toby (Precious Angel) Tobilone

The Lord He gave us eyes to cry whenever we feel sad;
The Lord He gave us lips to smile whenever we feel glad.

I smiled at your lovely funny face –
just knowing you made me glad.
I cried when you had gone to God –
missing you made me sad.
You were around eighteen to nineteen years old
and we'd known you just over two.
At 2.30pm on Saturday the 13th of August, 1994,
you came to us out of the blue.
At 1pm on Friday the 30th August, 1996
I knelt beside you and stroked you as you were put to sleep.
Now I'm crying my heart out endlessly –
for you I just weep and weep.

God keep you lovely Toby –
our dining room will be your shrine . . .
I called you 'daft-looking' dog affectionately –
but loving you all the time.
'If dogs have a Heaven,' sang Elvis,
well, my Heaven was being with you.
All who had known you had loved you –
there won't be another like you.

Oh God, how we all miss Toby
now he is no longer here;
Cradle him gently and whisper
'We love you' softly into his ear.

His every step was a falter;
his every fall was a sigh;
His every look was my altar –
there's no way to say goodbye.

Creamy-white hairs still on the carpet
and clinging to the velour-drapes;
As I vacuum round it's heart-break –
not a bit of difference makes.

For his hairs cling round the nozzle
and climb up the long black tube;
His image imprinted everywhere,
whatever my emotional mood.

Toby is here in his hair-brush
and on my black/blue dress;
He is here in my heart –
I never felt such pain and stress!

A most-lovable peaceable creature
who put everybody at ease;
As adorable as gentle Jesus –
all he ever did was try to please.

But near the end everything seemed to go wrong,
for old-age had come over him slowly;
Though his poor back legs were never strong –
always weak and spindly.

So, dear Toby,
As you left your stain on the carpet
and did things you would not once do,
I could never be angry or upset
for God was calling for you.

You barked when you entered our garden
throwing your head back with your one-note sound:
Woof! Woof! Woof! Woof! You'd call to the wild wind,
and I'd call, but you wouldn't look round.

For you were deaf when I tried to say 'No' to you –
your hearing had gone with your youth . . .
Miss your bark and your greeting 'hello' now –
miss your everything, that is the truth.

When you came to use
we didn't know that your name was Toby
so, I called you Angel at the start.
Got to love the name of Toby –
didn't know you'd fill my heart.

Yet, I either trod on your paws or tripped over you –
for you were always under my feet!
You ate all you were given quite readily –
especially your biscuits with meat.

Your tablets were never a problem
with butter around them for treat;
And your cod liver oil capsules
you ate like a vacuum on feet.

But, you never once grabbed from the hand
or gobbled, or threatened in any way;
You were always our gentle sweet Toby
who loved watching children at play.

Though you barked you could be trusted
with infants and pets, and creatures quite small;
There was never a moment of panic –
I could leave you safely with all.

And when something threatened you –
you just turned and slowly walked away,
Though you protected me from a gang of boys
who had menaced me badly one day.

Tom Tom often clawed at your eyes from the table
and Lucy Locket went for your nose now and then;
But you just stood there and took it –
not a bit of hate was in you,
no thoughts to get your own back on them.

You'd call me down in the night to remove
little Princess Puss Puss from your bed,
And Wendy Woo and Scruffy do miss you
and I miss the hairs that you shed.

The birds I rescued, you'd sniff at,
and now and then they'd peck at your nose,
But not once did you ever turn on them –
you stood like an angel in pose.

The children all loved you like crazy,
the adults smiled at your funny shape,
For your back-half was wasting and floppy –
but to me you were perfectly great.

No one could ever take your place –
there was only one sweet, soppy face
With gentle eyes and gentle ways
and sad and sorrowful woeful gaze.

No more peaceable creature in the world could there be
Than was our darling, daft-looking-dog Toby.

Rest you now with the angels,
though you are still here in my heart
Your spirit is all around me – I can't let go –
can't let the thoughts of you depart.

Dear God, if I should go to Heaven,
let me be with those on Earth closest to me
And let one of them be our dear dog Toby,
then, in Heaven, so happy I'll be.

Mary Pauline Winter, née Coleman

The Crocodile

The crocodile was bored,
he had nothing to do.
Swimming in the river
He snapped at everybody
who got in his way,
showing his long teeth
to scare small animals.
'I'm going to give you a present,
a very large toothbrush.'
This will keep you busy
and give you a kind smile.

Noris D'Achille

Harmony And Celeste

I bought myself
Two guinea pigs
This was a first for me
I named
My new companions
Celeste and Harmony

I gave them both
A brand new home
One to share with me
I've gained myself
Two roomies
To keep me company

I sit with them
Most every day
Sharing inner thoughts
And listen to
The sounds they make
A garbled kind of talk

I watch them both
When eating
Munching on some hay
Running around
In circles
When excitedly they play

Huddled
Close together
Celeste and Harmony
My two new
Furry friends
Sharing life with me.

Barbara C Perkins

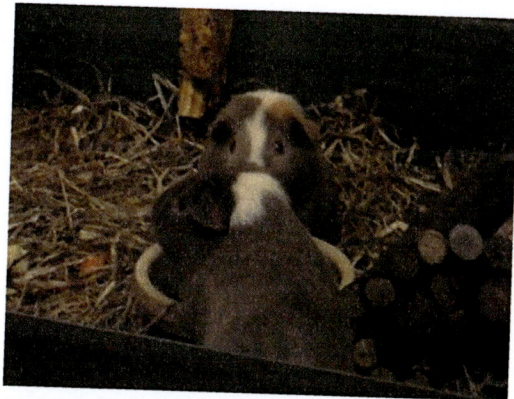

Ivory

The elephant is hunted for its ivory tusk,
the ivory tusks are sold and shipped all over the world.
Piano keys are made from elephant's ivory tusks,
paintings, signature seals and house signs,
are all made from hunted elephants' ivory tusks.
Even baby elephants are hunted for their tusks.
Ivory means 'dentine' which constitutes
the bulk of the teeth and tusks of elephants.
Elephants are known for their emotional intelligence,
Love and deep wisdom.

Aqeel Ali

Tom

A ginger Tom so tall and strong,
He sports dark waves upon his fur
That once went down his tail.
Great discussions on how he lost his fine tail
Was it on his nightly prowl
And got involved in a frightful brawl?
A great hunter is our mighty tom,
One could feel sorry for his prey.
Was it a mink or even a fox?
One less limb for him to lick
When Tom lost his precious tail

Margaret Gleeson Spanos

Ginger, Sheba And Billy The Kid

He is truly king of the castle
This ferocious feral cat, Ginger.
His queen, the black cat, Sheba
Who proudly strolls beside him.
They also have a human companion,
The runaway kid called Billy.
Streetwise, fearless and clever.
They live together in the twilight zone,
A derelict wasteland of ruined factories
And decaying 19th century tenements.
Frequented by addicts and outcasts.
They all sense something is coming,
Something powerful and truly evil.
An impending Hell mouth is opening,
An inter-dimensional tear invoked
Into the infamous netherworlds.
Were races of demon beings live
Who seek the fecundity of Earth.
Seeking the blood of beasts
And to feast on human souls
Gathered at the impending opening.
Two wildcats and the streetwise kid
Who will soon become super heroes.
Engendered as they now are
By the power of the high ones.
Aided by the archangel Michael
And a host of numinous beings.
God willing they'll make a winning team.
Thunderbolts wrench apart the sky's horizon
A dying sun sheds bloody fire on the scene.

John Pegg

Sampson

This tender caring little chap
Would come and sit upon my lap.
He knew each moment I was sad
Would come to me and make me glad.
At times when food was on the table
He waited close, knew I was able
To give him treats when he did beg
Then off to lay his sleepy head.
He touched my heart in every way
My lonely life was gone away.
This precious little dog, to me,
Became a comfort, for all to see.
He brought me smiles, but made me cry
The day I had to say goodbye.
When times were tough, was always there
He was an answer to my prayer.

Jackie Allingham

The Lonely Donkey

Danny the donkey was all alone
He had a large field and a barn that was home
His owners were kind but he was so sad
He needed a friend to make him feel glad

One day a man came to take him away
He didn't know where he was going to stay
He found himself looking out over the sea
He kicked up his heels and hee-hawed with glee.

He couldn't believe there were donkeys all round
For children to ride on for only a pound
With a child on his back he felt quite proud
He was patted and talked to and paraded around

At the end of the day he was glad of the rest
But he knew by morning he'd look his best
He'd be back on the beach whatever the weather
And he'd never be lonely again – not ever.

Mary Lunn

My Pet

My sweet, sweet lovely one
I give you love
That weighs a *ton*

You mean so much to me
I don't know where I would be
Always stay by my side
One, two, three
As I count looking for you
I think I've hit a breakthrough

With you always here
Never far, but always near
That's how much I love you
And you're my sweet pet
Never will anyone touch you
With a dirty, sharp-edged *net!*

Unbreen Shabnum Aziz

Little Bright Eyes - A True Story

As she opened the door
Kate stifled a roar
There was such a surprise
In front of eyes!

For all clean and bare
Just lying there
Were three strange plates
None of which was Kate's!

Through using the phone
Kate soon had them home
My mini shitzu
Knew a thing or two!

She had brought these plates
From the homes of her mates
She had used her brain
For personal gain.

Kate could not resist
Giving hugs and a kiss
My clever shitzu
Knew a thing or two!

Kathleen White

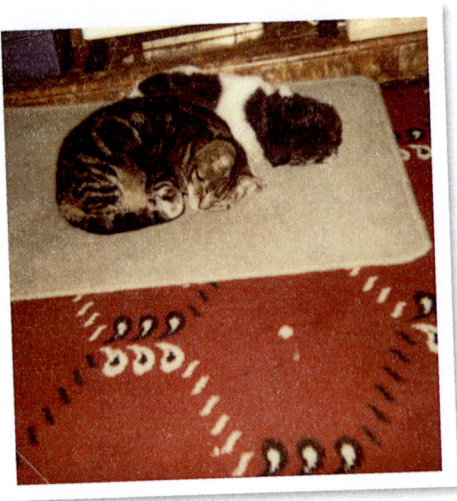

A Quiet Place

It's a quiet place, said he
Is where I want to be
Nothing too grand or spacious
But not under a tree
The birds woke me this morn
With their chorus just around dawn
So I stretched, gave a big yawn
And set off across the lawn
The dog must have heard it too
Because it attacked you know who
So I rolled into a ball
Then he could do nothing at all
My spikes must have stuck in his nose
So he wandered off wounded I suppose
My mind was in a whirl
When I began to slowly uncurl
And glancing around across the grass
I saw my dream retreat at last
I've found the perfect place
It's really ready-made
Down at the bottom of the garden
Right inside the shade
I think it's been a stool
For a toad or was it a frog
Although I'm not really cared
It's an ideal quiet place
For this tired old hedgehog.

David Holmes

The Circus Tiger

The circus of his life is over,
he was not able to put up a hit show.
Eyes raging with anger and disappointment,
as he took his final bow.
He had cost his masters,
indeed a pretty heavy sum.
For nurturing him they had to sacrifice,
many an evening's pleasant rum.
With every investment they made,
they built up more and more hope.
One day, all their efforts will pay,
and all their difficulties would elope.
Then came the long awaited day,
to introduce to the world 'the one'.
The stage was perfectly set,
millions of hearts to be won.
But he was not a performer,
the show was a total disaster.
Frightened, he ran back,
only to find rejection and hatred in eyes of the masters.
The lights were switched off,
the curtains were drawn.
He stood there as still as a stone,
not knowing where to run.
He kept waiting for his masters to fetch him,
for as long as he could remember.
He felt his breathing slow down,
and regretted his living before taking his final slumber.
The circus of his life is over,
he was not able to put up a hit show.
Eyes raging with anger and disappointment,
as he took his final bow.

Payal Rajguru

Charlie

Gone had the days of running and jumping, now all you did was a lot of stumbling
Your muzzle was now grey and your teeth all decay, but you knew you still had plenty of play
Reaching up on the kitchen tops, filling your face with our pork chops
Sticking your head in the bin and finding you couldn't get your whole body in
Contents all over the floor and a look of, you only wanted more
Your breath smelt of something quite foul and you often would let out a good, hearty howl
Sharing your hair with the rest of the home, was often an excuse to give you a good shampoo and foam
Airing your authority was a common occurrence, barking like it was a competition of total endurance
Alarming the postman as he knocked on the door, you were entitled after all, as you were one hundred and four!

Suzanne Paul

Flying Fish

Sitting by the sweet waters
As the cold rush hits my skin
I can feel Africa flowing throughout
Flowing out and in.

My rock chair is hot and firm
Heated by the midday sun
I am alone and yet I'm not
I am everyone.

The air is thick with peace
And I am still in my youth
Tranquil for the first time
While all the world rushes through.

As the waters pass in front of me
Connected to the Earth time by time
A silver fish with eyes so mighty
Through the water's surface pierced
Into the air, brave new world and back again
Just like that, and back again.

Natalie Williams

Muddy Paws

There's one thing I surely know,
It's 1am and out she'll go
To tease the neighbour's Labrador,
Eat two birds and bring back four
And if I dare to pass a treat,
She'd rather bite my hands and feet!
She has all day to hog my bed
But takes it late at night instead.
When my fingers smell like bacon
She assumes they're for the taking,
But when I see those amber eyes
My love for her I can't disguise
A cold wet nose and silky fur
I love to hear my moggy purr.

Heather Harwood

Tomcat, Tomcat

Tomcat, tomcat learning flight
Ginger, striped and two feet white
Leaping from a tree unheard
A furry, whiskered, wingless bird

Tomcat, tomcat stalking mice
Patient, still, sharp claws the price
Waiting, watching, scenting prey
Unwary rodent softly slay

Tomcat, tomcat on the lawn
Sun beats down, you lie and yawn
Your yoga leg raised in the air
You wash and stretch without a care

Tomcat, tomcat loves to fight
Awesome, snarling, squealing bite
Pummelled feet and swinging paw
Gaping wounds from hammered claw

Tomcat, tomcat won that night
Black cat ran from ginger fright
Tufts of fur and swollen ear
Ginger, swipe and show no fear

Tomcat, tomcat hungry now
Purring, calling, he knows how
Fresh-filled dish with food once more
Vital fuel for cat-of-war

Tomcat, tomcat by the fire
Green eyes drifting, dark desire
Gazing, lazing, logs of heat
Warming smell from padded feet

Tomcat, tomcat in the night
Ginger striped and two feet white
You disappear when darkness falls
And never come when Daddy calls

Tomcat, tomcat got it made
Another life you wouldn't trade
A cat-like bliss, supreme, sublime
No stress, no work, no sweat, no time

Awesome.

Robin Martin-Oliver

Alfie Angel

A rich pallet of colours vastly spread,
through the grounds on that autumnal day.
Your halo was silent, but we held hope,
close to our broken hearts.

Stout little highland terrier, handsome chap,
when you came to say hello,
we melted into your blanket,
of white, soft fur.

Alfie Angel, you came to our rescue.
Kindness, love and a lending ear.
Always close, paw in hand.
Never answered, but tried to understand.

Walks through seasons,
we share with joy.
Exploring, searching,
nose to the ground.

Barks protect us in the shadows
of the night.
Alfie Angel our bundle of happiness,
and sheer delight.
Since your arrival, life is sweet,
this household now complete.

Nicola Jean Holden

Laura Palmer And Audrey Horne

Charcoal Marans approach their task
Efficiently, I heard – and true, I found.
(This time last year, you numbered three;
We lost *Log Lady*, I think she was egg-bound.)

You take your cue from lengthened days,
The extra minutes undetectable
To human eyes, our blundering ways.
The weakest winter sun embraced in full.

Your combs so rubicund reveal
Fulfilment in the purpose of your kind;
Complete your resolute appeal
And leave the barren winter months behind.

I sometimes think we should talk more;
You bluster noisily when I come near
And stalk around within the fence –
I hold you sometimes, trying to counter fear

On both our parts. I must admit
To feeling apprehensive at the thought,
At first, of keeping you; you don't
Have fur, and cats aside, I'd never sought

Companionship from animals.
Yet something in the way you strut and seek
Out worms, or scraps of peel, or bread
Appeals to me; the way your beaks

Are jutting almost constantly
Towards the ground in hollow confidence
Gives me hope that all will work
Out well in life; my loyal, unknowing hens.

Jon Cooper

My Canine Friend

Described as man's best friend
A dopey expression to you he tries to send
Lively soul
Tail wagging
A language only known between man and friend
A friendship built forever
A walk in the park together
The only thing you can't see is the trust untold
And the secrets that won't be sold.

Stacey Hubbard

Track Cattle

A stopwatch snips the end of the race,
As runners, sprung by a gun, energy wrung,
Stand waiting, stopped by a mark on the ground,
In the measured lanes of the athletics world;
The race to nowhere; milking time over.

Robert Black

Dragon

This dragon can fly
Soaring high above mountains
High up in the sky

This dragon breathes fires
Bigger than you've ever seen
That you will admire

Great fire burning hot
Through anything it touches
Stop it? You cannot

Scales shining up high
Blinding all my enemies
Right before they die

They'll see majesty
Before I dismember them
I am bloodthirsty

I keep my respect
As a dragon proud and true
This you should expect

Creature of wisdom
More than you can ever know
Knowledge my kingdom

I am truly old
I have seen worlds come and go
Though my heart's not cold

I will always fly
And I will always breathe fire
High up in the sky.

Ahab Hamza

Panda Permutations

Pandas are cuddly, whitish and black
Fur a nice contrast
Feeling safe in the dark

Viewing their front face
They seem quite benign
Filling their own space
Not jumping in mine

But glancing from sideways
You can't gauge their sight
Staggering through their days
To reach certain height

Rolling in splendour
Relaxed friendly balls
With all permutations
Of where they might fall.

Tracy Allott

Sidney The Snail

Sammy was a little boy, maybe five or six
He didn't play with other kids, found it hard to mix
But he was a happy kid, his smile would never fail
Because he had a best friend, Sidney was a snail

This snail was a beauty, had a brightly coloured shell
He never made a nasty mess, never made a smell
He'd sit on Sammy's shoulder and laugh at Sammy's jokes
And when they were on Facebook he'd give him lots of pokes

He took his friend to McDonald's with laughter and with skips
But Sammy made a bad mistake – put salt on Sidney's chips.

Gary Wickson

Bulldog Badge

Since your love of the bulldog breed,
And my discovering two badges indeed
Told their worth on the Internet
Great, they may appreciate yet!
Ours were only on printed cloth,
Still, worth keeping for a future off,
Regimental insignia of a defunct corps,
So really not available any more,
Without enjoying extra cash
To cherish pets that cut a dash,
You went away to Dementia,
Your gift a pet for loving care.

Betty Bukall

Trim

I'm a black cat
A special cat
A ship's cat.
I was born on the Reliance
In 1799.
Of all my mother's kittens
I was the one most fine!
I'm a black cat
A special cat
A ship's cat.
I have four snow-white paws
And a white star on my chest.
There are many cats on board this ship.
The sailors like me best.
I'm a black cat
A special cat
A ship's cat.
When it's time for dinner
I don't eat with other cats.
I sit at table with the men.
I don't care for rats.
I have a special friend
And Matthew Flinders is his name.
He has called me Trim.
I think together we'll find fame.
I'm a black cat
A special cat
A ship's cat.
Matthew is a clever man.
He's sailed all round this land.
He's given it a name
And that's Australia – how grand!

Perhaps you have a cat at home.
Is it as fine as me?
Would it like to come on board
And sail upon the sea?

With a black cat
A special cat
A ship's cat.

Pat Simmons

Birds

What a lovely sound in the morning dawn
Birdsong in which they send their call
Be it the little blackbird in her nest
Or the robin with his striking, red breast
Returning home to where they belong
Laying eggs, awaiting their young
Be it a seagull on their way
That's how you know
You're at the seaside, that very day
But the bird
That's my favourite of all
Is my budgie
I know I'm home
When I hear
His call.

Emma-Louise Gardner

Python

I am your enemy
In deep disguise
Moving smooth
You can't hide
Delicious eyes
Hunger I need
I watch you slowly as you feed
Slithering all so close
I want you the most
I am one's self
One of the kind
A little prying mind
Good to find
Precious recipe
My sticky signs
Hope you don't have enough energy
To run and cry
Sexy complexion
I curl around your body
I squeeze and tug
Smother you in a hug
Curling concentric
Centre you like a spider would to a bug
No time for you to try
Fighting, you have no tribe
You give in a surrendering sigh
Slowly as you die
My scrumptious morphia
I bite into your veins
No longer will you feel any pain
Strangled into perfection
Now I must feed
Let me drink your nourishments with glee
Travelling down my neck in greed
Silky and cruel
Eating what's left of your broken wounds
Licking my lips, you've gone too soon
Satisfied success

Nothing really to confess
I move away swiftly
Disappearing with a hiss
Searching for the next menu
I am sure I wouldn't miss.

Emily Ryder

For Pebbles

Your beautiful eyes provoke the happiness which radiates my soul
A gentle touch of the paw your endearing devotion makes me whole
The soft strokes of your fur which caresses my skin
Gives me a lifelong contentment I'm feeling within
You're a partner so loyal the trust is in tow
A commitment to honour has eased us to grow
You sense when I'm lonely and feeling so down
You'll purr with a rhythm which echoes aloud
Cuddles to cherish and kisses we share
My feline companion who'll always be there
Your spirit shines brightly to lighten my days
My own shining star to guide me the way
The wiser quirks of age are beginning to show
If only one wish I'd make each year slow
Time is so precious I wish you could know
With each passing day the love forever flows
Until the day of your fate I'll continue to care
Rest assured, little angel, I'll always
Be there.

Kerry Webber

Farewell Spencer

Au revoir dear feline friend
Spencer, my favourite cat
Gone to join your namesake
Though never mine, I loved you
Sometimes looking after you
Missing you when you moved away
You seemed pleased to see me
Whenever I came to Devon to stay
My lap was open to your weight
Full length you liked to lie
Spread upwards with one paw
Gently touching my cheek.

Betty Gilman

Basil

Jumping on surfaces,
No more
Sleeping on laps,
That has ceased to exist.

Now you hide,
You run away,
Except when you're hungry
My sweet feline friend.

I may have been scratched by you,
You may have overheated my lap,
But I will always love you,
Dead or alive.

Morven Sara Cann

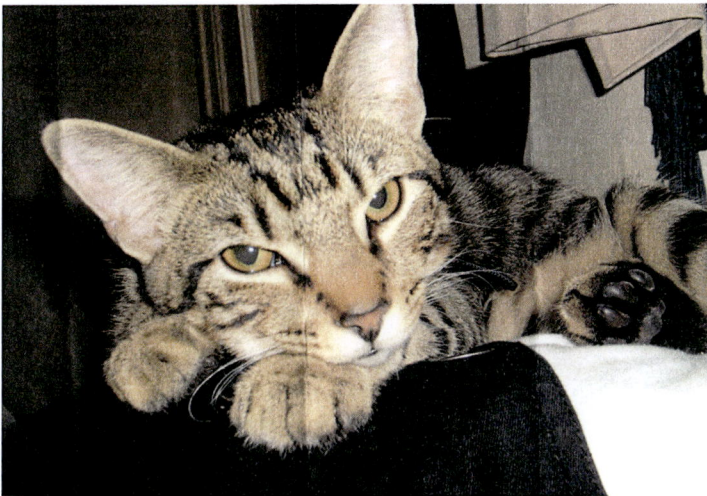

A Tail Of Disdain

Look now, here cat,
Now you're home
Permit me, will you, to pick a bone?

Your haughty reign here,
Must come to end,
Before it drives me round the bend.

Don't stare so at me,
Don't be so curt,
It pains me too that the truth may hurt.

This is it, see!
Though just begun,
Feel free to wash there with your tongue.

Hey! Don't mind me,
Clean bits best left unseen,
Oh! How you made poor old Granny scream!

And while we're at it,
Look over there,
And tell me please, whence comes that fur?

And here these paw prints on this table,
Hello real world!
And goodbye fable.

Remember you, a Christmas past,
When you had us all aghast,
To find you there amidst our feast,
Devouring turkey, filthy beast!

I wish I could say all ended there,
Hypnotised upon my chair,
But not enough you lick the plate,
Then before us all regurgitate.

Aunty now, is quite recovered,
Though it's quite apparent you're not so bothered,
She asked for you still, truth to tell,
She recommends you down a well.

Listen to me,
I won't repeat,
And stay right there upon that seat.

Not down there!
Pfffff, up you come,
Now pay attention, don't dare run.

Don't roll your eyes,
Nor frustrated glare,
C'mon Roomie, fair is fair!

Which takes me to the time of sleep,
When wakening I heard a tweet,
And turning snugly in my bed
I found my bird gift lying dead.

How I screamed and jumped with fright,
Which you mistook for my delight,
For there again upon the morrow,
Lay another lifeless sparrow.

Just bear with me,
I mean no slight,
But I'd rather gifts that don't take flight.

And while I hate to raise the question,
Indeed my business is your digestion,
So dinner times do not impress,
When you appear with trailing guests.

Nor turn your nose up at the fare,
I've little doubt you eat elsewhere,
So let's be frank, and let's be straight,
You must learn to appreciate.

No! Don't go wandering,
Don't curl up,
At least until this matter's shut.

Moving on then,
And next my seat,
Where you pose your regal feet.

Not long ago, beseeched to move,
Against my skin, claws carved a groove,
And in the hissing, heckled fight,
I believe someone did take a bite.

Then on retreating for relief,
Once more I felt those vengeful teeth,
The scars have healed, gone is the pain,
Yet ever fearful for my sane.

Oh! On the subject of your marks,
Upholstery is not for larks,
Munching paper or my plants,
Revoke at once this merry dance!

There, there now Puss,
All is said,
What now? Time that you were fed?

Twist and twirl about my feet,
Then directly for the street.

What I say, have you no reply?
Backward glancing with a half-closed eye,
And tail erect as proud as She,
Who dallied with the triumvirate three.

'My intention, minion, is to sup,
I'll be back for breakfast, so don't wait up.'

Shay Martin

Ryk And Tara

Tara, a German Shepherd, and Ryk, a King Charles Cavalier
Two animals so different who get on well together
Tara, the dominant one, lets Ryk know what she wants and he has to obey

Tara becomes excited when seeing a squirrel
Shouts excitedly to let me know where they are
Runs back and forwards wanting me to follow
Can chase a rabbit, or hare, for quite some miles
Never catching either but enjoys the chase
Loves the parks and the fields where the animals are
Talking to them as she talks to me
Shouting impatiently at me to hurry on for her walk but is
Quite happy for me to stand and talk on our way home
When in the car she excitedly tells me the way to the country parks
And is quiet on the return journey
Shouts for her dinner when she is hungry, asking for liver!
Sits, looking longingly at the cooker when chicken is cooking
She knows that treats will be forthcoming

Ryk, is quiet but very intelligent
Enjoys performing his 'tricks' for the children
Who have taught him to box, play dead and dance
Is always ready for his walks but must be kept on a leash
As he likes nothing better than to 'disappear'
Making his way into someone else's home to sit by their fire
He, like Tara, sits at the oven door awaiting his treat of chicken
But won't eat anything else apart from sausage
Loves being driven around and would prefer this to walking

Alas, both now have gone their separate ways
Tara visits occasionally but Ryk I have not sensed.

Margaret Monaghan

Fudge

We have the cutest hamster,
His fur is brown and white,
With little tufts above his ears,
He is a handsome sight.

Once within his hamster ball,
Fudge races round and round,
Then when playtime's over,
He's nowhere to be found.

We end up playing hide-and-seek,
And hunting high and low,
For back within his lovely cage,
He does not want to go.

Fudge escaped one evening,
He gave us such a scare,
Until we finally found him,
Behind our big armchair.

He didn't seem to notice,
The panic we'd been through,
But looked at us as if to say,
'What's wrong, what did I do?'

He tried escaping from his cage,
Until I secured that too,
I'm sure he sits there planning
The next escape he'll do.

If I forget his favourite treat,
He squeaks and squeaks until,
I place the treat within his paws,
Then he'll run off squeaking still.

Fudge loves his fluffy bedding,
Which he moves around a lot,
For he doesn't like his bedding,
Very long in the same spot.

We love our little hamster,
And his funny little ways,
For since he came to live with us,
He has brightened up our days.

Amanda-Jayne Lanceley

Huskies In The House!

Remy and Snowy. Unusual names I know,
But they're brilliant in the snow!
These names will soon be famous,
For these dogs are bold and shameless.
Snowy is white and lazy,
While Remy is brown and crazy!
Two huskies, both aged 11,
But to me they're my paradise and heaven!
Remy is an adventurous hound,
Escaped to a motorway,
And died when found.
But a vet managed to get his heart to pound,
And he is still with us to this day,
Racing around.
Snowy doesn't have a story to tell,
Apart from a hurt leg
From where he once fell.
These dogs sound like an odd pair,
But do you know what?
I don't care!

Molly Millar (9)

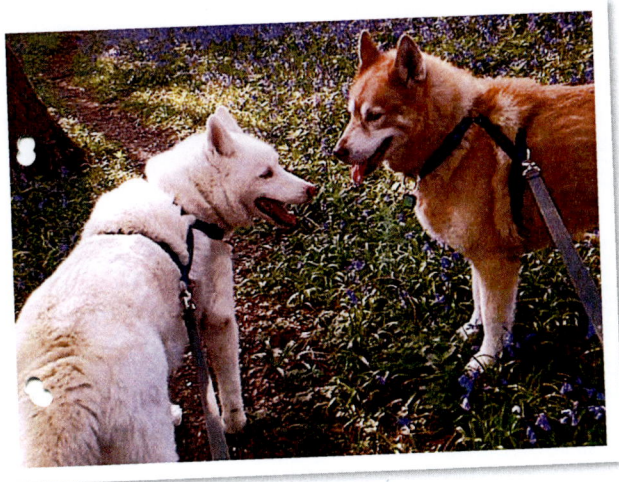

Mechanical Cat

The mechanical cat,
Is mostly black.

With levers to pull,
And buttons to press;
The mechanical cat,
Provides a life with no stress.

For a family of 2 to 23,
He did the washing and made the tea.

This is fantastic,
Thought the family of four;
As mechanical cat stood,
Cleaning the floor.

But as a drip dropped from the dripping drain,
It landed on his head and seeped to his brain.

He turned on his paws with a twinkle in his eye,
And swaggered to the table where the family ate pie.

Just as little Josie held a plate out for more,
The cat let out a magnificent roar.

This made Josie and the others take fright,
As the factory-formed cat became fixed in their sight.

Nuts and bolts pinged through the air,
As the family took shelter with growing despair.

The house became quiet,
There wasn't a peep,
As night turned to day,
On the family street.

The cat had morphed to a fifth family member,
And they all enjoyed their first December.

They ate lots of turkey, stuffing and more,
And didn't seem to worry about the dirty kitchen floor.

The family felt bad that they'd taken him for granted,
And that he slept on a shelf that was slightly slanted.

So they built an extension and added a room,
For the new family member to stare at the moon.

He lay and thought about life as a cat,
Cleaning and ironing and being shouted at.

He awoke the next morning bleary eyed,
As he heard a scuffle and howl outside.

It was his 13th birthday and he'd been bought a treat,
A dog called Otis who was eating the car seat.

His head rose and sniffed the air,
As he turned to the birthday boy with a mischievous glare.

The boy's first instincts were to turn and run
As the dog took chase as he thought it was fun;
He ran up a tree in an attempt to escape,
As Otis paced at an impatient rate.

The only way to get the boy down,
Was the fire brigade in the centre of town.

Needless to say, Otis had to go,
To a family down the road in the next row.

The boy used to hear him bark down the street,
As he sat on his purchase of a slanted seat.

He stared at the moon from his bedroom door,
As he knelt on his knees to clean his floor.

Simon McCann

Pet Or Pest?

He's fat and hairy with four short legs
He struts about and he always begs,
He can't bear birds and things like flies
He's always looking up to the skies,
Defending, yes, his family home
I don't think he would ever roam,
Tho' he is a nosy little tyke
And sometimes doesn't seem to hear,
When busy chasing or the like
And retreating when he gets too near.
He knows the sound of his master's voice
And whether or not he has a choice
To come straight back or just ignore
Then he just rolls over on the floor.
He always strives to be the first
Which sometimes proves to be a curse,
Pushing, jumping – under feet
He's always ready for a treat.
Rolling over, lying down, he never ever wears a frown,
Tho' he can sulk and turn away
Not speak to you the whole long day.
But when he smiles and wags his tail,
Although only a stump –
You know then he's forgiven you
For giving him the hump.
A hairy being with four short legs,
He steals into your heart,
A pet – a pest – whatever,
He belongs – he is a part.

June Johnson

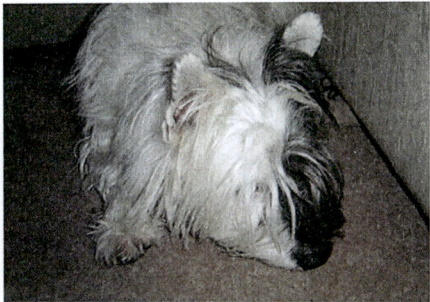
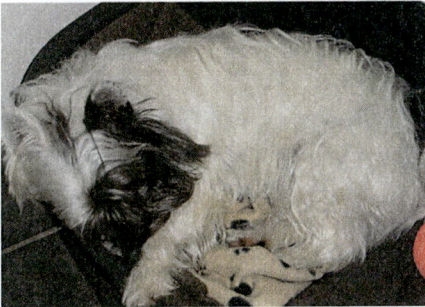

Magnificence

All trimmed up in the circus show
Ribbons, bows, flowers on the go
Showing off his shiny coat
No wonder his thoughts are to gloat.

Magnificent animal, the best
And beautiful, of course,
What other has his strength
And can't be beaten? It's the horse!

Whether it's trudging for the farmer
Or for royalty's ease
This old faithful
Is around to please.

He may be struggling
Running the races
Or he could be giving rides
To the joy in children's faces.

His versatility is endless
This lovely old favourite
His uses are numerous
He often takes the limelight.

Whether dragging coal bags
Or charging Red Indian
Aiding the cowboys and cavalry
It's all in a day's work for this bein'.

This so loyal servant of man
Animal of great use
So there is no call whatsoever
For any abuse.

Barbara Sherlow

Table Scraps

Blackie
The wonder dog
Was a one-time beast
With patience and temperament of Job
Willingly taking abuse
From four Brooklyn boys
A Labrador retriever
Who daily fetched
Our hearts
And carried them back
So gently clenched in his teeth
We never knew
He was
The master.

Jim Hart

Our Visitor

He arrived last harvest within a sheaf of corn
Unexpected but much welcome guest
His coat is honey fawn and button black eyes
Busy all day – no time to rest
Out and about – we hear – before dawn
No better place to build a nest
Pattering of feet near by the altar
Or scurrying between the pews
He's seldom seen – maybe by a few
That doesn't mean our guest is not about
They are all God's creatures – for sure
He's happy in new home – no doubt.

David Charles

My Cat, Freya

I have an awesome cat named Freya,
Whose hunting's a sensation;
The only thing that trumps this skill
Is her knack for calculation.

Her knowledge of maths outstanding:
Learned dons even sing her praise,
From Cambridge and Harvard and
Oxford and Yale! 'She's amazing!' one even says.

All honour her reputation
For arts so mathematical:
And her craft of dark equations
And their relevance to the practical.

She flummoxed Stephen Hawking once
On one renowned occasion
He gave in without reserve
To her algebraic persuasion.

I am not overstating the case
With surfeit hyperbole,
But she rivals Einstein and Nash and Feynman
And others in their league.

And with cunning she can reckon
With the most uncanny flair,
To the width of one of her whiskers,
The exact place for a lair.

It may be on the kitchen floor
Or on one of the steps of the stairs
Or some place we are sure to tread
Or a specially targeted chair

Where she can bring disorder
And massive disarray
And a frisson of excitement
To her humans' day:

But her random computations
And their sure veracity,
Suggest she's mastered chaos theory
And trigonometry.

For when one walks across the floor
Or needs a space to do
Some vital chore or needs a chair,
She's there with a 'howdy do'!

How does she know? we ask ourselves
And applaud skills so precise
But sometimes I wish she'd ditch her maths
For the art of hunting mice.

Christopher McDermott

Do Animals Go To Heaven?

Do animals go to Heaven
Way up in the sky
Do they go to that wondrous place
When it's their turn to die?
Will I when I get there
Be met by my old pets
Will my bitch, Jess, be angry with me
For her last walk to the vets?

Will they all come running towards me
As I walk past those golden gates
Gyp, Sally, Narvick, Sutcha, Heidi, Leana
Will we all again be mates?

Is Friday with the others
Waiting for year after year
Will they all wag their tails
When through the mist they see me appear?

Keith Coleman

Poppy

The cutest little kitten that I ever did see,
Her name is Poppy and she came to live with me,
With eyes so wide of amber and blue,
And fur so red and white stripes too,
She purrs real loud to show she's happy
And plays on her own if you let her be.

Her antics make us laugh and chuckle,
Running up your trousers to get your belt buckle,
Playing with marbles and laces and balls,
Climbing up curtains and even the walls,
Leaping from sofas to chairs and books,
Going to the toilet when nobody looks.

She's clean and fluffy and so much fun,
I'm so glad that I have won,
The love and trust of this furry little ball,
And now she's learned to come when I call.
Right now she's sleeping on the bed,
Curled right up, paws tucked under her head.

She looks so tiny and her fur's nice and shiny,
When having a nap she's really quiet,
But when she wakes up there will be a riot,
Peace will be shattered and toys will be scattered,
But we'll all be highly entertained,
And no one's pleasure will be feigned!

Deborah Price

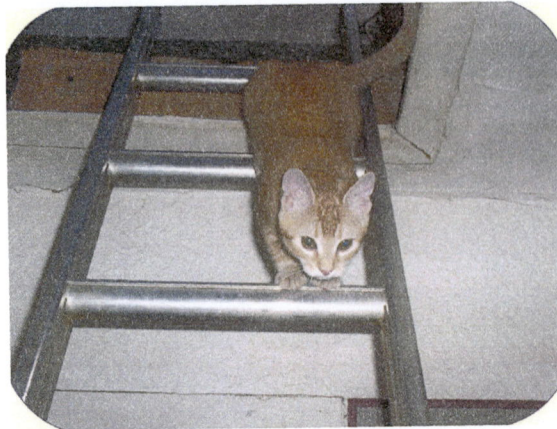

Yoko

Sleek, slender, mysterious and black,
Piercing eyes of emerald green,
The cutest little cat you have ever seen!

Whiskers made of fine wire,
A purr that sounds like a roaring fire!

Tapping 'George' with a furry paw,
I wonder what your little eyes really saw?

Put on Earth for such a little while,
With all your charm and your guile
We loved you little Yoko,
That's why we called you 'Yoko Poko'!

So be a good little pussy cat,
Chasing all God's mice in Heaven I bet,
To the sweetest pussy cat, we have ever met.

Suzanne Swift

My Wonderful Pets

I feed my goats carrots
And the goats smile at me,
Thanking me for their food
I offer to them.

I love the donkeys too,
You can see all my animals
As they silently gather around.

I take good care of them all,
So lovingly,
I bathe them and they love
To be bathed.

I do believe they were sent
From Heaven
And that I am their angel
Watching over them.

I make crafts with pictures
Of my animals,
And give them as presents
To family and friends.

My animals are my best friends
And they always love me.
I could never ask for a better friend
Than my pets.
They are my good luck charm.

Melanie Lynn Miller

Sandy At Rest

Soft, warm, cuddly an cute,
With big, bright eyes that melt your heart away.
A tiny little mite at my first sight of him,
Jumping this way and that onto my lap.
Now, as time went on growing so fast enchanting all,
My memories I here recall.
Down the years we've shared so much love and happiness,
Sometimes pain.
Yet nothing shall replace those bright bewitching eyes shining bright as the stars.

Anywhere I went he came too, my bed he would explore
And beside me snore . . .
Then snug, with me he would lie, looking at me with knowing eyes
And touching paw.

Reflecting on times now past, he, Sandy, will never be outclassed, special he'd be.
Each day of his life was filled with excitement from dawn to dusk each new day.
So what, he only had three legs but that was part of his charm
And alarm to some?
Thus 20 years flew by, then my furry friend sadly died,
At my side, how I cried.

Michael Counter

Bonnie And Clyde, Cheeky Grey Squirrels

Early hours of the morning
Just as the sun rose from his bed
Two naughty, cheeky grey squirrels
Came into my back garden
One I named Bonnie
The other I named Clyde
Just like the two outlaws Bonnie and Clyde
Long time ago in America
Decided to try out their luck
By trying to take nuts from the bird feeders

Bonnie tried first, balancing with her tail
That wrapped around the branch to steady herself
She tipped up the bird feeder and held it in her paws
And started to nibble at the nuts
In the bird feeder
Clyde came hopping along too upon
The ground and ran up the tree.
I opened my window and shouted
'Shoo, you little buggers!'
They did not take any notice of me
They hopped away as cheeky as ever as they came.
Then they were back again
Having another go at the bird feeders.
This time they both went up the tree
Again I shouted, 'Shoo!'

Clyde ran off, Bonnie stayed behind
And looked around
With a cheeky look upon her tiny, grey face.
As she ran back up the tree again
I shouted the third time until
I went hoarse.
She sat upon the ground staring at me
Through my bedroom window
She slowly made her way to the tree again
I looked at her and said, 'You dare!'
And guess what? Yep, you've got it!
She looked and ran back up the tree again.
There was nothing I could do
Just sit and watch them both
Through my bedroom window.

Bonnie and Clyde, those little outlaws
Of the squirrel world
O, those little cheeky grey squirrels.

Samantha Rose Whitworth

A Poem To Our Basil

Shiny, silky, floppy old ears,
Once again he's a pup going back thru the years,
Dreaming of the time when he was wild and free,
The hazy summertimes lying under the tree.

Walks by the riverside, throwing sticks, sparkling sky,
How he loved to run, coat and tail flying by,
But he's old now, strong legs have turned weak,
There's still a twinkle in his eye,
When I watch him from my seat.

Yes, still shiny, silky, floppy old ears,
Coming back here towards the years,
Where he is now, and will always be,
A very loveable and everlasting memory.

Yvette Clegg

Shula

She was a female who knew her mind
Within her breed, one of a kind.
And when at first I watched to see
I was so glad that she chose me.

When just a pup she was so cute
With long, black ears and tail minute,
A white blaze on the top of dome
Midst greys and black of true Blue Roan.

And when at school they said 'no brain'
She ruled the roost with some disdain,
And always put the males in place
For me that special 'sad look' face.

A loyal friend she proved to be,
So many happy hours with me.
She liked to walk and search for balls
Away from worried golfers' calls.

She always had an eye on food,
But mostly she was very good.
She'd sit and watch and hope perhaps
Her bowl would fill with tasty scraps.

What I would give to see her now
And hear her 'speak' to me, somehow.
I hope she knew I loved her so
I'm mortified she had to go.

Jo Robson

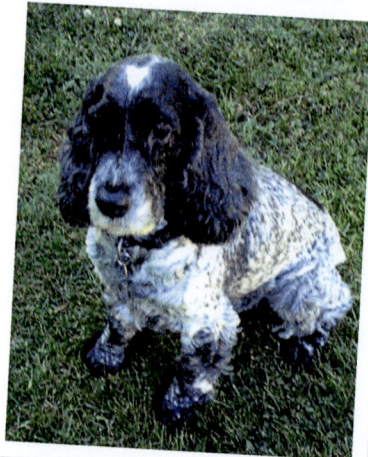

Sooty Is A Fighter

Sooty is our family pet
She has beautiful black velvet fur
Unfortunately she had to go to the vet
She knows she's loved and we're always there

The vet examined her
Sooty had a lump just under her skin
They were gentle because they do care
Our poor rabbit's fur is still thin

It was decided she had to have an operation
And her fur had to be shaved
Her family waited in anticipation
She was well behaved

We were told it was cancer
And they had to remove two of her teats
Luckily she is still hopping around taking her chances
Afterwards the wound was stitched up tidy and neat

They gave her, her medication
And we told her we'd get her through this
We thanked the vet for their dedication
As we took her home and gave her a loving kiss

Now Sooty gives everyone she meets
She's still a young bun
A gentle lick to greet
Sometimes around the living room she'll jump and run

Tina Rooney

My Dog Puck

My dear old dog is a faithful friend
And has been for many a year,
A pal upon whom I could always depend
Whether the skies were dark or clear.

His is not so quick, or so nimble now,
As he was for the days gone by,
But his old tail wags when he's near me
And affection fills his eyes.

The time will come (may it yet be long!)
When me and my dog must part,
But I'll ever remember his comradeship
With a glad and grateful heart.

And whether it late or early be,
That the parting day draws nigh,
I'll tend and comfort his all I can,
Till the time to say 'goodbye'.

For a human friend might have failed me just
When I needed one the most,
But my dear old dog thro thick and thin,
Was always at friendship post.

His bark of welcome was full of glee,
Whenever I homeward came,
And whenever I scolded or whether be caress'd,
He was ever to me the same.

Sammy Michael Davis

On Safari

I visited a park, a safari park,
I partook the ride in my car,
Those chimpanzees tore my wing mirrors off,
What mischievous monkeys they are!

They swung up and down on my windscreen wipers,
Inflicting them physical abuse,
Then they scratched their heads trying to work out
The best way to force them loose.

A llama alarmed me, it spat in my eye,
Impeding my vision immensely,
Then a troop of camels passing by
Took a dislike to me intensely.

I'd refrained from winding my windows down,
Anymore than an inch or two,
But the llama and camels spat me down,
Drenching me through and through.

A mighty crash fair rocked my car,
As a rhinoceros rammed it precariously,
The elephants trumpeted in seventeen bars
And the hyenas laughed hilariously.

A lioness scratched at my passenger door,
A second one lay on my bonnet.
I questioned what else might lie in store,
My car, whatever would become of it?

Well, there I was just sitting there,
Thinking of all things bad,
While those hyenas laughed at my despair,
More than ever they had.

A ranger arrived to rescue me,
He had a few words to say.
Safari parks?
Again?
Not me,
Though the animals had a wonderful day!

Peter T Ridgway

If They Could Speak . . .

If they could only speak
The fox could tell us how it loves the chase
And then the stag, gaping wide-mouthed at the saw-toothed pack
Might boast with his last gasping breath
How dignified and noble was his end

And chimp 4321, resplendent in her crown of thorns
Could tell us just how proud she feels
As the steel bites deep into her aching head
That she, the last survivor of her tribe
Must die to save five billion human lives;
How willingly she makes the sacrifice
So our endangered species might survive . . .

God help the animals. What sins have they
That must be died for every day?

Dory Phillips

Spot

I remember when I thought it was a sheep,
All big and fluffy,
With coat that was so deep,
My fingers vanished all into the fur,
When stroking him,
But my eyes did blur.

I recall I often had a ride,
With my dear nan walking by my side,
To catch me, just in case I slipped to fall,
If he should bolt,
Whene'er his name was called.

He was the biggest dog,
Taller than me,
A giant,
But protective as could be,
Wherever I went,
Old Spot would plod along,
His bark was fierce,
His paws were huge,
His body strong.

Marcy Wilcox

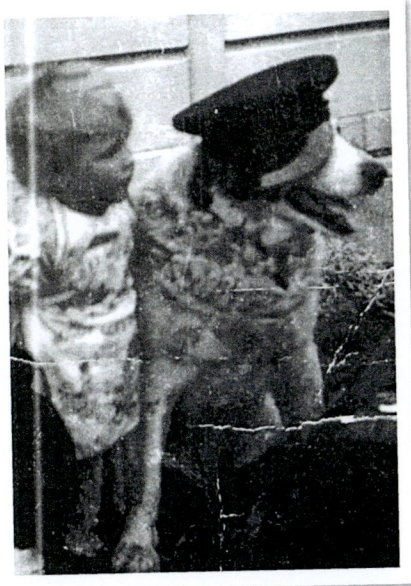

Susy The House Ghost

Clouds hang like rags around the moon,
A squall has passed to give a mottled night,
The garden sighs and comes into her own
Under a pale starlight.

The watching, listening house withdraws
Her shutters open to the cool night sky
Too painfully aware
The house ghost passes by.

With noiseless footfall to her haunts
Of yesterday – the long and languid hours
Spent in pursuit of butterflies
Among wind pollinated flowers.

Soft fur at angles to the wind
She leaps into a favourite tree,
With star-bright eyes this gentle spirit cat
Now watches over me.

A white and russet shadow falls
Dancing ahead or at a window seen,
Briefly my empty void fills with
A warm silence that causes me no pain.

Comes a day soon when dawn breaks
And the sky will speak of fair weather,
Then we shall leave, she and I
For the last time – and together.

Frances M Searle

A Pigeon's Passing

Just how it was you managed to complete
Our home, in some small way, I'm not quite sure;
But now you're gone, it's clear we must endure
No little passing; for, you could compete
With any in this house and, though devoid
Of certain skills and aptitudes inspired,
And though, at times, your antics made us tired,
Your love and trust, in measure unalloyed,
Were cherished as unchanging, as a child
Had come and banished care away, I say,
As sun and spring had made a perfect day,
And May herself, a queen, had softly smiled . . .
And, though the autumn leaf be bound to fall,
We'll miss you Pidge, we mean it – from us all!

Alan Gore

Adopted By A Cat

When we first met our cat, we thought it a stray,
Thin and bedraggled, unsociable, fierce,
We watered and fed it, it would then slink away,
But back in the evening to be fed and to see us.
It wanted food and attention, but no stroking or fuss,
Then off to its bed with a flick of its tail.
If you offered affection, it would just sit and cuss,
A tiny, but feisty feline female,
Our neighbours told us it wasn't a stray,
But lived in a house just up the hill,
With two other cats, much bigger, they say,
The owners, a couple, both worked at the mill.
We put up some posters and our phone number too
And waited to hear if what we'd heard could be right.
As luck would have it, it was perfectly true.
So, we decided not to feed or water it that night.
We ourselves went out to visit some friends
And didn't get back until very late.
We'd wedged up the cat flap with some odds and ends,
She could never get in with the flap in that state!
But when we got home, there, to our surprise,
On the couch, sat a very persistent old cat,
Pleading with us with translucent eyes,
For milk and food and maybe a pat.
Although very late, we sent it back home,
And with a heavy conscience, we went off to bed,
Having first secured the flap with some foam.
We awoke to a noise that would waken the dead.
It woke up the neighbours on either side,
Even though they were both partly deaf.
The cat charged about, howled and cried,
And hardly stopped to take a deep breath.
We had little option but to let the cat in,
Where it has stayed, considering us home.
A smile on its face said 'I knew I would win',
It is now very loving with no need to roam.

Bernard Newman

Extra Special

Well, here they are,
My two little girls,
Nothing fancy, no ribbons or curls,
Just faithful companions,
Constant and true,
Without them, well just what would I do.

A walk, a chat, a biscuit, a treat,
Two better friends, I've yet to meet.

Because of them, I'm never lonely,
Just extra special,
That's Molly and Rosie.

Jacqueline Claire Davies

Caddy

Expectant but patient he waits at the gate,
A walk through the woods with my companion and mate.
His profile so regal as his nose finds a breeze,
At the gateway that leads through the woods and the trees.

Like a pistol he's off as I open the locks,
His nose to the ground on the scent of a fox.
Down the path he swiftly snakes his way,
His tail in rhythm to his gait-like sway.

This is our happiest time of all,
For me and my chocolate Labrador.
No matter the weather, come rain or shine,
This is our moment, Caddy's and mine.

Racing ahead catching smells in the air,
Glancing back now and then to check I'm still there.
The birds in the trees herald our approach,
Into their world we respectfully encroach.

Our eyes full of sparkle as we make our way home,
He waits at the gate so I'm never alone.
In the warmth of the fire we both take a nap,
He stretches beside me, his head in my lap.

At dinner he really could be much calmer,
He devours his food like a frenzied piranha.
Then watches intently each mouthful I eat,
Hoping for morsels to fall at his feet.

He looks in my eyes and a warmth fills my soul,
His love is reflected there, unconditionally whole.
What he gives to my life I cannot measure,
How can I repay his infinite pleasure?

Each night his protective presence is there,
Ensconced in his basket without a care.
I wonder if, in his dreamlike state,
He stands and waits for me at the gate?

He's there to greet me when I walk through the door,
His feet tapping on the kitchen floor.
Nuzzling my hand whenever I'm down,
Eyes so sad but a warm honey-brown.

My dear lad, Caddy, he is an old boy now,
Time seems to have passed us by somehow,
I need to tell him before it's too late,
'Caddy remember to wait for each other at the gate.'

Jean Wilson

Sally

I have a friend, we've shared our lives for many happy years,
Rarely have there been cross words, never any tears.
We enjoy each other's company more than words can tell,
Our love is just like man and wife, or that of boy for girl.

She stays at home while I'm at work and never does complain,
If I come in a little late, because I've missed my train.
We go to bed together when all is safely locked,
But not before we've had a walk, then watched the old square box!

Sally is no lady, as you have surely guessed,
She's just a little mongrel bitch, one of the very best.
We're getting on in years now, me and my old Sal,
But never have I had before, a finer little pal.

Peter Mahoney

Our Mutual Friend

A chestnut gelding standing tall
Thought it fun to make me fall
He'd gallop fast and start to buck
And leave me sprawled there in the muck!
He stopped at the water one fine day
And with bubbles blowing, there I lay
Flat out on the river bed
Water flowing past my head.
Another day, a sharp turn right
Gave me such an awful fright
As I landed in that prickly gorse
I'm sure I saw a smiling horse!
He gently nudged me as if to say
It's time we were going on our way
'I think I'll walk if you don't mind,
A prickle's stuck in my behind.'
But as the months turned to a year
It suddenly seemed so very clear
I'd earned respect and now his friend
And we'd be together 'til the end.
His velvet muzzle nudged my arm
He would no longer cause me harm
Our first rosette took pride of place;
The pin-board's now run out of space.
We're now a team, my friend and I
And tears of pride are what I cry
He's winning shows and looks so haughty
No one would know he'd been so naughty!
But that was 'til my sister tried
To get on Butan for a ride
I saw the glint back in his eye
I think I know what he will try!

Elizabeth A Green

My Boy Rio

In life you didn't have a good start,
Having to see you like that broke my heart.
I had to get you away from that place,
I just fell in love with that kind face.
Your eyes showing me the inside of your soul,
You'd been through so much for a little foal.
I saved you and in return you saved me,
And we both began to feel so much more free.
Your roan coat now glistens in the sun,
And you and I are free to have fun.
I love you with everything in my heart,
I know nothing in this world can ever keep us apart.

Georgia Swain

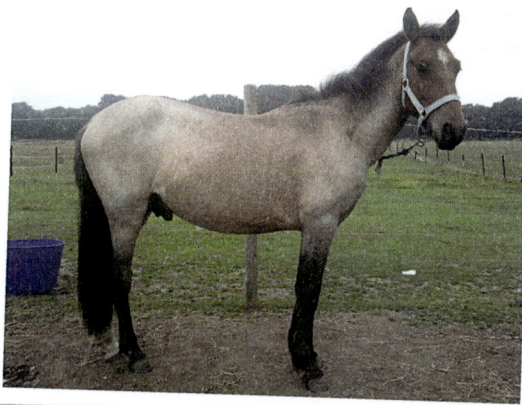

Dogs In The Night

Where have the dogs gone?
In the wonderful sky
Barking and howling
In the moonlight.

Stars in the sky
Friends with the dog
I always know why.

They jump to meet
And bark to greet
But they are hunting
To be free.

Jumping up and down
Howling in the night
Being brave in the moonlight
They are going home.

Then they wake up
But they were in the soft basket
Dreaming in the sky.

Saumya Nath

Apples And Chips

We've got crab-apple trees in our garden,
But we haven't got that many crabs,
We get loads of little apples, about one inch across,
Our chipmunks thought they were all up for grabs.

To see a chipmunk squatting on his haunches,
A small crab-apple gripped between his paws,
His smiling little face showed such enjoyment,
As did the chomping sound of tiny jaws.

We haven't got our chipmunks any longer,
But still our trees produce a load of fruit,
The grass-box on our lawn mower gets full of apple sauce,
Cos crab-apples get squishy underfoot!

Mick Nash

A Bird

I rise with the thermals,
Sing on the treetops.
Take heart in my surroundings,
Feel the air beneath my wings.
Life for me is a breath of fire,
Beautiful, wondrous and unimaginable.
There are no questions for me,
I live, therefore I strive,
And find beauty in my surroundings.

Why there are no questions,
Is because my life is full and rich,
I live without want,
Fear or grief.
My life is forever complete.
I am the bird in the sun,
The silhouette of everlasting light
And the sun is all around me.

Eilidh Fergusson (16)

The Mouse House

A little mouse lives in a little house beneath my bedroom window
And when some seed to the birds I feed
Falls on the floor, outside the door of the little mouse outside my house,
A whiskered nose twitches and clicks all the switches
To scurry the mouse straight out of its house
To gorge on the store of abundance galore!

Then appetite sated (long enough waited)
The little mouse outside *my* house
With rounded tummy and feeling rather yummy
Retires to bed and, may it be said,
Dreams of seeds falling like leaves, from the jug of the mug
Who lives in the house above *my* house,
Clearly not knowing that all his to and froing
Is bestowing a mouse with free board and a house
But better, better yet, with all the food it can get!

Henry Powell

Enzo, My Dobermann

Enzo, my Dobermann, a black and tan beauty
Came into our lives aged two
He's a big softie at heart
With so much love to impart
He's also an excellent guard dog
He has a loud, deep bark.

He has a comforter blanket
Which he sucks with all his might
There's dust on every surface but
His amusing antics are truly a sight!

He loves capers with my grandson
They're a lively pair indeed
It's really hard to decide
Which one should have a collar and lead!

His pet hate is cats so
Their paths must never cross!
He's not so brave, however
When confronted by my heavy horse.

He follows me like a shadow
So protective is he
A more thoughtful, faithful friend
There could certainly never be.

A home is not complete
Without a dog I say
It has no life about it
Although tidy it will stay!

Joan Catherine Igesund

Jemima Love

I have a little dog, Jemima is her name,
Since she came into my life, it's never been the same.
Every day her large brown eyes,
Gaze at me and seem to say,
Come on Mum, let's have a game,
It's a lovely sunny day.

Off down to the park we go,
We usually take her ball,
Sometimes we take her dumbbell,
But she likes that least of all.
She associates it with classes,
Where she had to come to call,
When she was young and puppyish,
That was no fun at all.

I love my little Jemima,
Without her I'd be lost,
She's my companion and my minder,
And I never count the cost.
The pleasure she gives me alone,
Is worth every plaything, toy or bone.

Gillian Grover

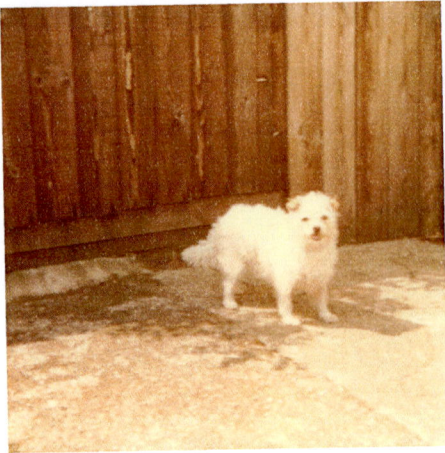

Stop It, Roger!

Roger's our rabbit.
He's white and grey.
We feed him rabbit nuggets and hay.
He hops round the garden
and chews up the decking
Chewing's his forte.
It's doing my head in!
My wishing well has chunks in its side
shaped like rabbit gnashers, deep and wide.
My plants are gone. All digested!
A bunny chew? He's not interested!
He's eaten my washing on the line!
I tell him off, he thinks it's fine.
He's eaten my dustpan, the brush too!
Stand still too long and he will eat you!
I've threatened the vets
to take out his chompers.
A rabbit with no teeth? Nah, that's bonkers!
I guess I'll just let him destroy all my stuff
and suffer more damage from one ball of fluff.
He's still only little, finding his way.
Just hope I can get him to eat more hay!

Andrea Roberts

Happy Hannah Fluff Fluff

Fluffy brown beauty, striped quite unique
Needing a home not far to seek
I'd fed the litter and watched her grow
We bonded quite quickly, she seemed to know
I needed her trust, she needed my love
A fair exchange, a gift from above
I've had so much happiness from this beautiful cat
Apart from her gifts, the odd mouse or rat
She's nearly ten, it's hard to believe
Come holiday time she's difficult to leave
Life without you I can't comprehend
Thank you, Hannah, my faithful friend.

Catherine Hislop

Untitled

Caged in behind silver bars
Look at me swinging to and fro.
I may imitate every word you say –
But I'm much smarter than that.
Flying around . . . always on the go
Pecking at my feed.
Look at my bright coloured coat –
You can't catch me!
I watch your every move
Every day when you pray.
Look at me a little closer
Read my thoughts today.

Jagdeesh Sokhal

The A To Z In Wildlife

Ants said, 'Come on, let's get going'
Bee replied, 'OK' and started humming
Cockroach halted and began slumming
Donkey told him, 'Don't be an ass'
Elephant stopped to eat more grass
Frog croaked feeling high-hearted
Giraffe neck went up when elephant farted
Hippo went swimming through his own dung
Iguana caught a fly by flick of its tongue
Jaguar was having its lunch
Kangaroo gave dingo a punch
Llama got the hump
Mouse at a corn stump
Nurse shark healed its fin
Octopus got stuck in a tin
Porpoise jumped and was made to beg
Quail sat there and laid an egg
Rabbits ate carrots and corn
Salmon went upstream ready to spawn
Tuna swam majestic in the sea
Umbrella bird hung in the tree
Vulture went scavenging over the land
X-ray fish went skimming the sand
Zebra brought up the rear of the band.

Gerald McNulty

A Mask Of Deception

Is this a face of innocence or the Devil in disguise?
Well, behind the darkest mask is where this secret lies.
Lead you into a false pretence never knowing if it's all pretend,
And then she bit my ear!
This little pup, so cute and so young
Doesn't know the difference, does not know any better,
Then she bit my wife's bum.
This puppy runs us ragged, this puppy bleeds us dry,
Expensive taste for the little miss,
But we can't deny her big brown eyes.
Excitable, to say the least, she can't be trusted off her leash.
The little husky wants to run far and wide.
Playful and sweet and a strange fetish for feet
She can't be the Devil in disguise?
Then when walking with the wife,
The sight of a ginger cat made her burst to life
And pull my wife to the floor.
Yelling through the window to me,
'The little pup has gone!' shocked me!
Then shocked us both to find her in the back garden
Sat next to her favourite ball.

Marc D Brown

My Best Friend

A distant shadow on the morning dew,
A hazy silhouette, black upon blue.
A gentle beast picks up pace,
Bounding towards you full of grace.

Once no more than pathetic and sad,
Abandoned, unwanted, we welcomed him glad.
We watched him grow from day to day,
A noble leader emerged, from this otherwise stray.

His features unique, his temperament mild,
Protective and trusted, round any small child.
His placid nature made him anyone's friend,
He'll remain by my side, till his days should end.

Our bond was created from love and respect
So devoted was he, I'm forever in debt.
My admiration for him shall never lower,
I introduce you to my best friend . . . *Noah.*

Louise McCall

On The Tiles

Tonight was murder committed.
The same MO.
Caught from behind in lacerated agony,
The corpse denied a bed on the cool tiles of the morgue.
While vagrant murderers bear witness in silent approval,
Late night revellers, on their own hot night out on the tiles,
Pass by, in drunken ignorance of her escape
To remorseless sanctuary with me.
Her guilty accomplice.

Earlier,
Street lights gloomed the moon's cool blue arrival.
That super trooper spreading the stacks
In two-dimensional expansion over the roof tiles.
Similarly extended, the vagrant murderers await,
Admission free, indolent yet eager,
Her entrance on the stage.

Inscrutable pout, she twitched her denied desire
And itchy irritation stepped her sexy sashay, towards me.
Tart, I thought.
She flicked, insistent at my obedience
And rubbed her cheek against mine,
Perfuming once more her domination.
And I? In meek submission, I opened the door.
Slipping loose the black-cloaked ingrate to murder.

Alert in silent anticipation, her audience perks up
To her strut strut strutting,
Their perfect night on the tiles requiring only
A naïve stage stooge, to be cast as victim.

Sniffed under the super trooper, he tippy-toed from the stony wings
And gasped, shock-eyed, as she,
Fierce,
Pinned him flat.
Gobgawked and terrorshriked,
Surprised death pricks hard then harder,
As she eats him bloody bone-crunching, from the legs up.

As if outraged,
Her disturbed audience rebels, head stiffed and forward
To that vamp's studied pretence in ignorance, which waited,
Before hissed defiance allowed escape
Under cover of noisy revellers,
Oblivious to the dramatic performance.

As her crying at the door betrayed her fear of discovery,
So my desperate dash to the door, mine as guilty accomplice.
In and safe, in true gratitude and devotion,
Her kiss, slow and gently rasped on my nose,
Passes the fragrance of death,
And ensures submission for one more night.
She lays down in my lap to lick herself clean.
Tomorrow of course, I shall let her out on the tiles again.

Richard Hayter

The Parrot

I am a parrot,
Flying up high,
I am a parrot,
In the blue sky.

I am a parrot,
Happy as can be,
I am a parrot,
Listen to me.

I am a parrot,
Beautiful, bold and free,
I am a parrot,
So come and see.

I am a parrot,
Hiding in the trees,
I am a parrot,
Yes, that's me.

Paige Wheeler (11)

The Cat Dog

You go out in the rain and then you snuggle in my bed
Or sit waiting up high just to jump on my head
You drink out of the toilet because you think you're a dog
When in all honesty you're my little mog.

You run around in circles to try and catch your tail
Always in a fight it's obvious you're male
But at the end of the day when you cuddle up with me
You are the best cat you ever could be.

Dana Andersen

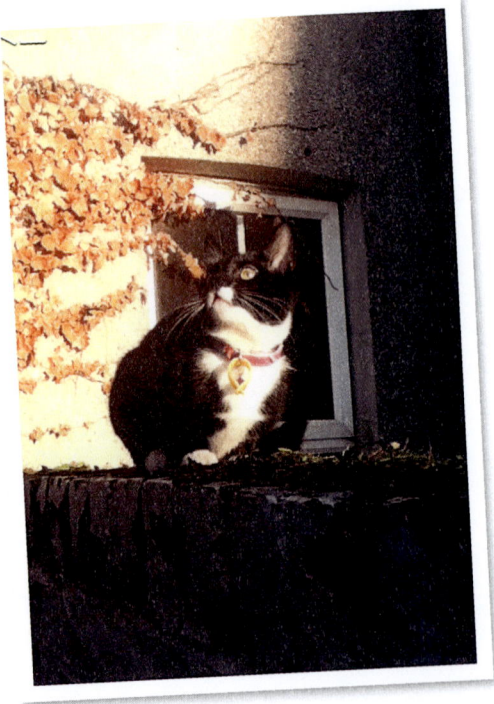

Your Tail Did Wag

You tail did wag, eyes shone bright, with key turning in door of home
Whimpering, barking as to say, I've been waiting here all alone
Standing up pawing, head on side, breathing breathless, excited shaking
Time for walking had arrived, eyeing dog lead on back door for taking
You'd run at the door, jump up, mid air, turn around, back legs kicking
With lead off the door, dropping to floor, growling at, pink tongue licking

A dog lead, no good hanging there, need to jump up and get it
The desire to go out, the sight of me, was what made his world tick
You were black and white, born of sheepdog and shaggy terrier
With short legs, fur covering your eyes, attractive, none prettier
Once the lead was attached, your excitement was no less abated
Running to the front door, jumping up, anticipation, needing sedating

Then we were out, him, tugging on lead, I wondering who's in charge?
Fast to parkland, past houses, under bridge, following path by river barge
Reaching the park grass, as far as could see, off with lead, travelling light
With speed he'd run, ears pinned back, a landscape dot, a bullet in flight
I would run with him, his tongue pink and out, happiness plenty evident
If human he would have grinned, exhilarating freedom, heaven sent

His name was Skip, a loyal friend, happy, engaging disposition in place
Pleased to see me, especially when preparing his food, leaving not a trace
Would turn full circle and bark anticipating the food that was to come
Knowing the opening of a tin, a signal for what would end up in his tum
I wish, looking back, I made more of my time with him, dear old Skip
Remember fondly, fourteen years, many times we went for a running trip

In his fourteenth year he became ill, not eating, getting slower
No longer able to go out and run, with little strength or power
His sight no longer good, he was coming to the end of life's journey
Distressing to watch, decisions on action had to be made firmly
Wrapping him up in a Scotch plaid blanket, carried in arms a gentle deed
Death left a blanket, noisy silent barking, on the door, a hanging dog lead.

Ron Constant

Unexpected

Whilst harvesting sweet corn,
One bright morn,
A jackdaw flew onto my boot,
Pursuit
Undoing my boot lace
Unable to chase it away.

It tugging at loose cotton,
On my trouser leg bottoms.
A wild bird so tame,
Its one aim,
Undoing my boot lace,
Pulling cotton threads
Out my trouser leg bottoms.

Threw a handful of sweet corn seed,
On pathway.
At long last,
The Jackdaw hopped off my boot
To feed on sweet corn seed.
Then flew into the sky
Without a leave or by.

Bryan G Clarke

King Freddy The Best

I remember it well, the very first day.
You a lively little pup and me a sucker for those eyes.
But in the car I knew I'd hit the jackpot, my all-time canine prize.
Known by many names . . .
Freddy, Fredriko, Pongo, stop that! And even popcorn dog.
You, my furry little friend, my chum, my amusement, my cuddle blanket, my rock.
Six am you serve as my furry alarm clock.
Awoken from a deep slumber to wet kisses galore.
I know what you're after, to be let out of the back door.
You make your entrance, put on a show.
Your behind wagging in the air, saying, 'I'm here! Let it be known!'
A strange one you are, your eating has me aghast.
But when the felines are let loose, bark of disdain as you make it to the plate. Fast.
Tail wagging nineteen to the dozen, mother yells, 'Stop that, buster!'
Your tail the perfect duster.
'Freddy, come here!' You know when not to come near!
Alas, I shouldn't have looked into those huge eyes,
I can never be mad, but with you that's no surprise.
When you're bemused, I know too well,
For there's always a funny way to tell.
That small mouth of yours morphs into a wonky line.
No fear of losing you, that Chaplin moustache, those floppy ears, that wonky mouth.
Yes, that dog is mine.
No fear my cavalier, debonair friend.
For you I will always have time to spend.
You're worth a thousand handbags and glad rags, yes sir.
Everything about you from your never-ending affection to the smell of your fur.
Strolling along together, lead in hand.
It's always as if everything I say, you understand.
The reason you're diamond is because you listen and never talk.
I can rant and rave and you never think me crazy,
Provided I take you for a walk.
They say through history that you're a fine breed, a blue blood,
Indeed, that's how you appear when walking delicately through the mud.
My Cavalier King Charles so dandy,
Always willing me to have a toy handy.
Always by my side, your loyalty prevails.
For you your name I will always hail.

No doubt about this one, through thick and thin and even fog.
I can promise you this; you'll always be top dog.

Emily Davison

H Is For Happiness

After all these years of faithfulness
I've been and gone and done it!
I've fallen for another
With a love that's *not* platonic.
I only have to look at him
And my heart skips a beat,
At last I've found excitement,
Know what it is to feel complete!

I do still love my husband
In a way, I always will.
But *he* won't give me what I want
Whereas my new love will.
Of course my new man
Is much younger
And he does have much more hair.
It never used to bother me
I didn't really care.

But as we lie together
And I caress his tousled hair
I understand the difference
Between a mane that isn't there.
My every move he watches
With his dark, seductive eyes
How could I think of leaving him?
This thought I agonise.

My new love is more active
Doesn't sleep and snore all day.
He's always happy – not a grouch
Like the one who's here to stay.
Like I said, I love my husband
And I wouldn't kick him out
I'm far too fond of that old git
Even though he makes me shout.

My new love restores the feelings
That I thought were long-since lost.
He doesn't question what I've bought
And how much it had cost.
He loves me if I'm naked
Or if I'm dressed up to the nines
Whereas my husband
Thinks I'm wrinkled –
Laughs as he counts the lines.

I watch my handsome new love
As he roams from tree to tree
His sturdy torso straight and true
As he lifts his leg to wee.
That precious dog has shown me
What love is all about
And I've found another manly being
That I just can't live without!

Rochelle Butters

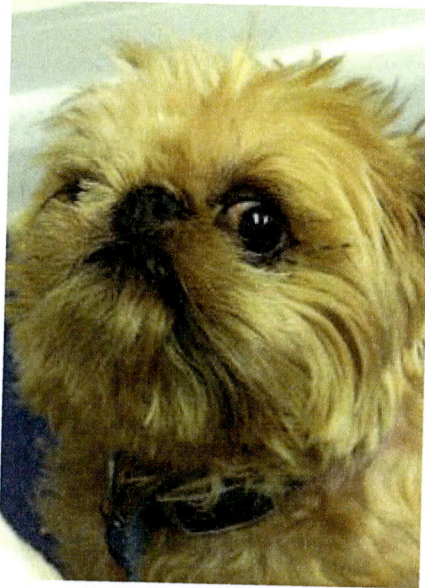

Sanctuary

The donkeys graze or browse or drowse in summer sun,
In fields above the sea.
Retired or rescued spend this last lease of their life in
Sanctuary and tranquility.
On windy days the donkeys run to greet, their necks across the gate.
Your troubles must be left behind.
Observant eyes and ears and eager noses wait,
They're urgent to communicate, insistent for your mind.

The timid ones, who have known harsher times, stand far,
Look longingly, view and review.
Their trust comes slowly as the summer air and must be delicately earned.

If you are patient, wait and wait, and wait,
As though testing ice upon the pool,
Nose tentative, eyes wide and questioning,
They come, and ultimately gently lean, to demonstrate that there is trust in you.

In winter barn's pervasive donkey warmth
Is peace of mind; and, strangely, of spirit
From their innate ability
To bring you, in their sanctuary, tranquility.

Deirdre Golden

To Own A Cat

Oh what of antics of animals
The cats the dogs in households,
And whether to have the bother
Of ownership for life of one.

So to own a friendly cat can be
Magic in a way for the owner,
As a cat can go and come daily
Only needing a warm home and food.

So a cat that I have presently
Has asked to be called familiarly,
'Miss Kitten' not any other name
As she says she has no kittens.

So to respect a pooch, a cat really
And to watch her come and go daily,
See her sleep and snore and then be
Still the idlesome one in house daily.

Pamela Poole

Josh

I'm 20 years old
A black and white cat
With attitude at the front
And scruffy tail at the back
I'll fight with all cats
That venture into my patch
With hissing and clawing
Flying fur just a scratch (on my head)
I bring in the insects
Of all different sorts
Especially the ones
That leap and cavort
She goes OMG
It's a flea, it's a flea
I look at her sweetly
And think it's not me
I cannot remember if I've eaten or not
I slurp up my water
No manners I've got
My hip gives me gyp
When I climb on the bench
And survey all the birds
That perch on the fence
My mind is still active
But my body can't follow
You're safe where you are
Only Whiskas I swallow
I sleep and I eat
And sunbathe my belly
I'm a couch potato
Without even a telly!

Wendy Marsh

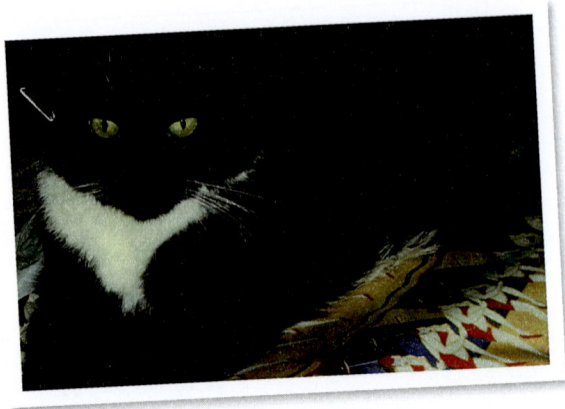

Birdie Hop

As she hops around her metal cage
She lifts her claw and gives a wave
Her laugh comes out as a high-pitched squawk
As she regains her balance from her birdie walk
Her bright yellow feathers are like spring flowers
Hence the name Daffodil, found in April showers
All alone in the dark, so we brought her home
Where she could get her food from a little glass dome
And she pecks at it and drinks her water
Staring at us, while the seed she does slaughter
Her sounds wake me up in the morning
But without her my life would be boring
And forever and always my budgie will be top
As she will continue her birdie hop.

Shaye Goodenough

Me And My Cockatiel

My cockatiel Charlie is the best friend I've ever had
I love him so much and I know with him I'll never be alone
He always cheers me up whenever I'm feeling sad
All I want is for him to know with me he'll always have a home
When I saw him at the pet shop I knew he was the one for me
He was the one I wanted and nothing else could change my mind
That day I vowed 'I'm going to show him what love is, he will see'
He is the perfect pet for me he's always so cute and so very kind
He flies onto my shoulder and begins to nibble my ear
He whistles at me to remind me that he's there and will always be
That's when I know I love him and he loves me, it's very clear
It used to be he and it used to be me but now we're together it will always be we.

Bethany Nunn

Rocky

His greeting every morning
As his eyes light up with joy,
Lifting up his head, wagging his tail,
Licking my hands and face!
As I call him 'darling boy',
He jumps down to the floor,
Showing the happiness of a new day –
    Once more!

He really makes an awful fuss
When people come to call;
He greets them all in silence, tail a-wag,
Expecting their attention, a game of ball.
Only barking if the doorbell rings,
But greeting most of them as friends,
He'll lie down eventually –
    Enjoying company!

He has a towel for rainy days,
To wipe his muddy feet;
To dry his fur or rub his tail,
But the game you cannot beat
Is playing at 'bull fights'
Or towel 'tug o' war',
Or hanging by his teeth –
    Or 'Blindman's Buff'.

Once the towel is hung away
Then onto other things –
A thirsty drink, a crunchy rusk,
Or even sitting staring at his bowl
Telling me he's hungry!
He dashes with me to the fridge
To see what's hiding there –
    All expectant!

He loves to sleep rolled on his back
With legs all bent and floppy,
Or puppy-like with legs behind,
Looking at us all soppy!
Head leaned on paws out front,
Or regal like a lion . . .
Wondering whether to play –
    Or go to sleep!

At night he jumps up in his chair,
Knows it's time for bed;
I blow a kiss, turn out the light
And nothing more is said.
He knows the house will soon be quiet
And all will be asleep,
He heaves a sigh and snuggles down –
    With confidence . . .

That morning will be
Another joyous day!

Donoveen R Alcock

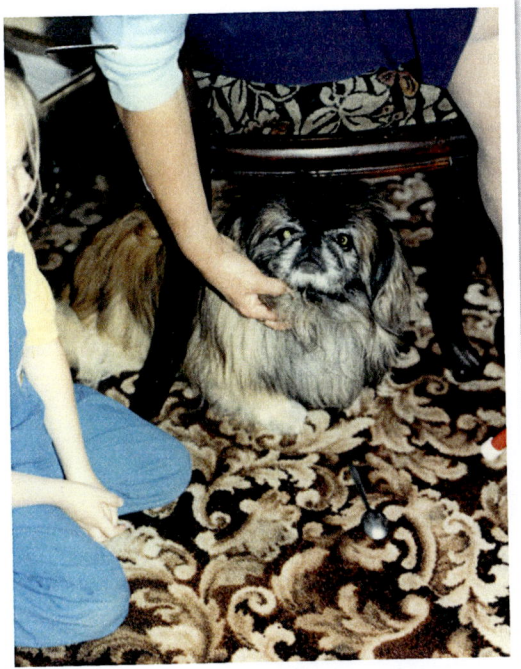

Love Conquers All

You lay in my arms that hazy autumn day
The car that hit you sped away
The vet looked at me
No words to say, eyes a misty grey
I'd better take him away
I looked down in despair
My tears of love mingled on his bloodstained fur
Suddenly, his paw touched my face
I felt as if God had given him an inner strength
If he has to die I'll do it my way
With loving care took him home
Weeks turned to spring
One eye gone, I put him on my garden lawn
I'm very proud of this now beautiful cat
Looking like Nelson, all he needs is a hat.

Barbara Posner

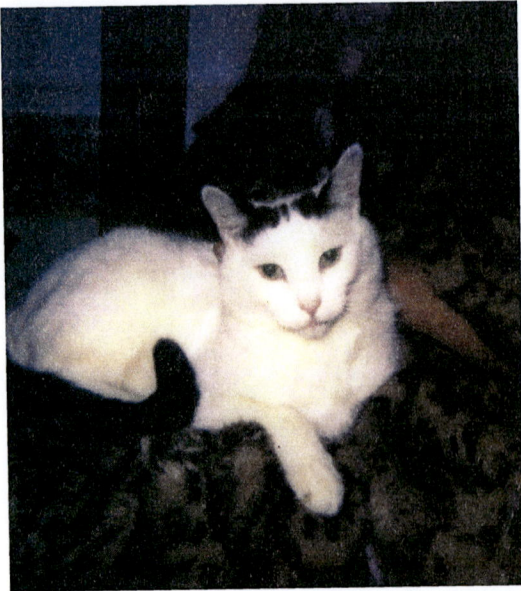

Felix

I am a hunter,
I always stalk my prey,
Then bring it home,
Day after day.

I sit in wait,
For a tasty treat,
The giants put it down,
For me to eat.

No one messes with me,
I am a king,
Annoying other creatures,
Is my favourite thing.

I have my land,
I leave my mark,
I patrol it religiously,
Usually after dark.

The people that see me,
Think I look so cute,
I am wary of them,
So away I shoot.

I have my favourites,
I never let them down,
When I am around,
They never have to frown.

I may seem rough,
But me and my owners are together,
We love each other
And we always will – forever.

Charlotte Eleanor Lucy Mellor

Old Age

I'm a feline geriatric, but my coat is still shiny and black
But sitting her in the window I can't help looking back
To the days when I was a kitten, when the world was full of fun
When my mother and I in the days gone by
Chased rabbits and mice on the run.

My father they say he was ugly
A monster all shiny and black,
Always feeding and fighting for what it was worth,
With a big, jagged scar on his back.

They say he got it one autumn
When he was chasing a toad
He forgot to look left and forgot to look right
As he chased it across the road.

He woke up at the veterinary surgeon's
Who lived quite near in the town
He snarled at the man bending over him
In his cap and his mask and his gown.

'What's the matter with me?' growled my father
'I'm feeling all stiff and I'm sick.'
'That's right,' said the veterinary surgeon
'And you'd better get better quick.'

'For once let this be a warning
Next time you chase a toad
Look left and look right and prick up your ears
Before you cross the road.'

So the old man got himself better
But life was never the same
No more feeding and fighting and growling at vets
No more chasing or playing a game.

Now I sit here just like the old man
With my coat still shiny and black
But like all feline geriatrics
All I can do is look back.

Ernst Wilhelm Peters

Fauna

Reliever of stress just by a stroke,
Makes you concerned, makes you joke.

Big dark eyes peer out wanting more,
Fetching a stick, by the seashore.

Perched on a swing, singing out loud,
Our owners are, ever so proud.

I can get grumpy if you neglect,
I'm very choosy I like to select.

You look forward to seeing me,
I like to curl up, on your knee.

I chew things I shouldn't touch,
Some are kept warm in a hutch.

Whiskers long, whiskers short
Shouldn't do that, I often get caught.

A long, expressive tail, a twitch,
Sometimes I can be a bit of a bitch.

Paws, my claws, my nose and eyes,
Knows my reward, knows my prize.

I preen my feathers or lick my fur,
I sing, bark or squeak or maybe a purr.

I will love you for all of my life,
Friends come and go, even the wife.

Master and friend, it always gets blurred,
Never ignored and rarely deferred.

So much power that loyalty brings,
It's hard to decipher which one is king.

Meia Allegranza

Modes

My dog, called Shade, has certain modes
Which she switches between.
One moment she will be in Play,
The next she'll be in Sleep.

When nature calls, she's up at once
And bouncing all around.
This is what we call Walk mode,
When she won't let you sit down.

When she's out, her business done
(That's called her Poo mode),
She gets it in her head to run
Like lightning down the road.

When home, she'll lie on sofa top
And stare out the window pane.
She'll count people out of the house
Then count them in again.

When we're packing for our holidays
And loading up the car,
She'll go into Anxious mode
Whether going near or far.

She doesn't understand the car,
What it is or how it drives,
How can she be standing still
When the world is flashing by?

She pants and whines all of the way
And her ears, they stand on end.
When out, she rushes far away
From this box she can't comprehend.

The stress will send her into Sleep,
Bio stasis practically.
Curled up in a content black ball,
Head resting on her knee.

The noise she makes when she's in Sleep
Is like a purring cat.
It makes the room feel warm and safe
When you hear her snore like that.

Anna Hands

The Listener

He's in every lunchtime, without fail, ready for a well deserved thirst-quenching ale
The landlord looks forward to his visit – 'Hello there Ben, the usual is it?'
He even has his own special chair, set aside – 'Ooh no, you can't sit there!'
He observes all the goings on, keeps himself to himself, bothers no one
Listens intently to the incessant chatter, says not a word, but it doesn't mater
'Would you care for a crisp? How 'bout a pork scratching?'
One's thrown but he misses, he's no good at catching

His eyesight's going but his hearing's acute, he's as gentle as a lamb,
not an aggressive brute
Never judgmental, never critical, keeps out of arguments, religious and political
His only contribution to conversation is a yawn
(Out of fatigue only, not boredom, it's sworn)
He'll nod in agreement, scratching his ear, having downed the last of his beer
Secrets and confessions to him they'll disclose
Though out of their business he'll keep his nose

Never spreads malicious gossip, never pries
It must be those warm, kind, big brown eyes
He's the one who won't betray a trust
To shake him warmly by the hand is a must
For he is everybody's friend, although a penny he'll never spend
With his grubby collar and old fur coat,
He's instantly recognised, a lovely bloke

Everyone wants to make a fuss of him,
The takings have even increased because of him
This is not down to the amount of ale he consumes,
But because that expression when he listens speaks volumes
He's a diehard regular, always friendly
He's a Yorkshire terrier, and his name is Benji

Andy MacDonald

Morning Traffic

The morning awaken with frantic haste
Awaiting breakfast, so time shall not be a waste
Purring and pawing, trampling on my chest
Making fresh new holes in my bedtime vest

Nudging me side to side with a furry head
Wishing me with innocence to leave my bed
A leg is out of the covers and the rush begins
Like a shark through the door just minus the fins

Shuffling and shunting is heard down the stairs
Past the scratched wallpaper with no cares
Fumbling sounds on the kitchen floor
Before I even reach the bedroom door

Halfway down the staircase scratching my chin and hair
Little critters peeking just to see if I'm still there
The sudden rush through the door now I'm down
Swarming through my feet round and round

With a morbid look as I take out the food
The kitty looks up rather confused
I look down to see a sly look on the face of the puss
With a comical face behind whiskers
Wondering why all the fuss!

Matthew Carr

A Dog Named Sid

There is a dog named Sid and he is very small,
It doesn't matter who you are, he loves to play a trick,
Like when you throw a ball upstairs to him,
He'll throw it back with a kick.
When we visit him, he greets us happily,
People all around him seem to love him immediately,
He's funny and affectionate,
Although he picks his likes,
Some people he takes too,
Some he dislikes,
So he is very happy in his environment,
And when he goes out for walks,
He especially likes the pet shop,
Where he goes from time to time,
They make such a fuss of him,
It's poetry in rhyme.
So we can't wait for our next visit there,
To see him once more,
And watch him jump from upstairs,
Down upon my lap,
And there he sits and has a nap.

Iris Crew

Alfie Puss - Tells His Tale

I think it was a special occasion
Nice smells were in the air,
It made me get up and prowl around
Out of my cosy chair,
That big noisy thing in the corner,
Wasn't making a sound
And all the family were laughing and joking
Just sat around.
I went exploring behind this big black thing,
Wires to step over, I really had a fling,
When leaping onto the top of it,
I could see my folks
Laughing and pointing at me! Was I the butt of their jokes?
No! They were making shooing noises, but
'Master' getting cross!
I slid down, peeped out from the side,
Tail up, to show who's boss.
I was doing no harm, I pad about with care,
Oh, but here comes Master, I'd better beware!
He's got this angry red face on,
He's shouting, 'Get down, now!'
If he comes closer, I'll scratch him and how!
Still, I'd better 'beat it', but others seem
To be smiling with glee,
Wow! I'm off, he's throwing his slipper at me!

Barbara Buckley

I May Decide To Reside With You

'I may decide to reside with you,' said Lady Tips one day.
'You must understand my needs and wants for me to agree to stay.
I'll let you know what tasks to do and how I like my tea.
We'll be just fine as long as you can just defer to me.
The house will be mine during my stay, so try to understand,
I like to roam, I like to sleep, but seldom lend a hand.
My previous servants have gone away; I suppose they deserve a break,
But mark my words, when they return, no more liberties they'll take.
I am a lady, through and through, but I do try to be kind,
But off they've gone, around the world, and left me here behind.
So do try hard to make my stay as pleasant as you can.
I'm sure, by the end, you'll be my friend and *numero uno* fan.'
PS Je ne regret chien.

Graham Hayden

For Sherman, The Rottweiler: Part Two

I made it into 'Animal Antics 2010' but then again, that was then.
My working days have come to an end,
I'm no longer around to be man's best friend.
My master's laughter I shall miss,
As much as all those days of bliss.
Broken hearts I leave behind
But hope some day that they will find.
Happiness for all their years,
And wipe away those running tears.
I had the chance to live with the best,
And now have laid myself to rest.
RIP Big Lad.

Stephen Wright

Who Are We?

My sister and I have a comfortable life
Easy going, no trouble or strife
We can sleep all day, stay out all night
And sometimes we have a real good fight
Our home is like a four-star-hotel
We get looked after so very well
Or meals are put in front of us, we just have to eat
We sit by the fire and lap up the heat
Sometimes a place on the settee we find
With a warm seat that someone has left behind
Then there's the fuss when, on laps, we sit
We're stroked and pampered for a bit
Out in the garden we have such fun
Chasing the birds, my, how they run!
Then there's the loose leaves, in the breeze they flit
To catch them we have to jump high, we're really fit!
We walk the fence and annoy the dog next door
Then jump on the roof and then to the floor
Back indoors all tired and spent
We climb in our beds and lie all content
And tomorrow, instead of roaming the house
We'll both go out and catch us a mouse
Or climb a few trees, we're good at that
Yes, you've guessed, we're two tabby cats!

Jan Collingwood

My Parrot And Me

My parrot and me love to play,
He eats his food on a tray.
My parrot loves to swing and slide,
Which he does every day.

My parrot is a cheeky bird,
And he loves to read his book of words.
His feathers are very bright,
They look attractive in my sight.
He has wings that are very pretty,
When he flies they stand out in the city.

My parrot and me are very close,
We even share the same toast.
He likes to eat carrot and peas,
Whenever he does he offers it to me.

My parrot is very sweet,
When I be sad he does and tweets,
He cares for me
As I do to him.
My parrot is a very good pet,
But we struggle while going to the vet.

Zabreen Busharat

Daisy! – A Present From Heaven

She came into our shattered lives To help us carry on,
A Springer puppy, Heaven sent,
To fill our lives with love:
With her little black mask
And white flash down her nose
Long, whippy white tail
And black spotted toes.
When we wake in the morning
She's there by our side,
Asking for cuddles
With those soulful brown eyes.
She climbs into our laps
And snuzzles right in,
Pushing her head
Right up under our chins!
She makes us laugh
As she pounces and prances,
Enriching our lives
As she dabbles and dances.
She runs like a greyhound
Up on the Downs,
Gay as a lark
As she dashes around.
She jumps over the waves
And she snorkels for stones,
Digs deep in the sand
On the beach near our home.
She's helped us learn
To live life again,
Our dotty wee Daisy –
A present from Heaven.

Kim Thompson

262

Mystic Cat

Fleet of foot,
She padded softly,
Turning here,
Looking there
Green eyes, bright
Staring in the dark
Camouflaged
By the night
Slinky cat
Coming home
Time to stop
Her midnight roam
Black as pitch
This feline witch
Casts her spell
Purring like a kitten
Until your human heart
Is smitten
And on the bed
She will lay
Sleeping softly
Till end of day
Then padding once more
She'll slip
Out of the door
For her next
Midnight mission.

T D Whaley

Tabby

I am Cat, the Hunter
I am strong and fleet of paw.
My ears are cocked, one back, one forth
As I stretch out on the floor,
But my yellow eyes drift closed
And I emit a gentle snore.

I am Cat, the Hunter.
My claws a fierce array.
The blackbirds and the robins
All view them with dismay.
But their feathers won't be ruffled
By a sight of them today.

I am Cat, the Hunter.
My teeth a wicked snare.
I dream a thrilling dream
Of how I stalk and trap and tear.
But while I dream, I give a purr
Without my being aware.

I am Cat, the Hunter.
Independent. Walking tall.
I *could* be in the garden,
But I'm lying in the hall.
The heater's right beside me.
(Comfort never starts to pall.)

I am Cat, the Hunter.
A tiger, fearsome to the end.
I don't expect mere humans
To begin to comprehend
How the wild beast in their living room
May sometimes be a friend.

Lorraine Coverley

Man's Best Friend

We've got a dog called Roger
Who thinks he's one of us
If you try to put him out at night
He just kicks up a fuss.
He won't sleep without pyjamas
And it's quite beyond belief
That just before he goes to bed
He goes to clean his teeth.

Mike Richardson

A Dog's Life

All washed and spry, I came to Edward's place,
And wrote a note, his hostess, a grandmother
To keep for him, then undertook to bother,
Whose dog was an old maid, she said, with grace.
His bed was a bare mattress, on which lay
Some things at which I had no right to look,
But from which my eye indirectly took
A single man's depression, and dismay.
I waited half an hour at his gate,
Then wandered round the Red Square until late,
Among sparse crowds that struggled to have fun.
Commemorating Russia's victory,
They had two rockets, while some soldiery
Lined up, yet stood at ease, and had no gun.

Dominic King

A Bee

The bee flutters day after day,
Finding nectar without delay.
She takes the nectar to the queen bee,
And then she's happy as far as I see.

A bee enjoys making honey,
(Especially on a day that's sunny!)
We all like honey I see,
So clap your hands and praise the bee!

I have to say a bee gets tired,
But they never get retired!
They enjoy their job so now we say,
Hip, hip, hooray!

Abigail Biddle

Trixie

The time has come to say goodbye
To hold you tight, while it's still light.

I've loved you so much, Trixie,
What an amazing 19 years we had.

Now you can enjoy the sun, for evermore.
Lie on fresh green grass, every day.
Watching birds flying up above.

I still can't believe I've lost you too,
But I have peace in my heart knowing;
You will be with your big sister
On rainbow bridge.
My girls joined together in eternal sleep.

My heart will always love you.
My arms will always long to hold you.
In my thoughts you will always stay,
Until the end of time.

Heather Wilson

Ptolemy

Aha! There's Ptolly, lumbering from a bush,
Not very fast, but with determination,
An interested gleam in his old eyes.
Ptolly's a tortoise, bought at market, French,
My present on the day I reached thirteen.
(You'll understand that this was . . . long ago.)

Hungry, old Ptol? Let's see what I can find.
I know you're not fanatic about salad.
You don't conform to common lore, declaring:
'All tortoises are slow and relish lettuce.'
He thrusts his pointed head into tomato,
Snaps at a cooked and succulent green bean,
Extending a long neck, deliciously.
He likes to let me stroke his scaly throat.

Today he's ready for attention, for some sport.
'Watch him!' I cry triumphantly. 'See how
He clambers o'er the rungs of garden chairs,
More than a good inch high above the grass!'
The grown-ups laugh indulgently: 'A circus trick!'

I love my tortoise's firm, rounded shell,
So intricately patterned; love his face.
Such joy, to be surprised when he appears –
Not every day: he likes to feel he's rare.

A friend's big, playful dog one day upturns him,
Investigating this odd, moving stone.
Ptolly withdraws head, tail and legs inside his shell.
Convinced he's dead, I leave in tears for school.
But no! once danger's past, my Ptolemy relives
And makes for undergrowth, his dignity intact.

Another autumn comes. No more tomatoes!
The summer warmth is gone, yet still the days are mild.
Ptolly disappears to hibernate.
No warning reaches him of greater cold to come,
No frost alarms him, whispering 'Bury deeper!'
And with the following spring, after a normal winter,
We fail to find our friend who's gone to sleep
In leaves or earth too shallow for protection.
Ptolly has gone, he will awake no more.

Katharine Holmstrom

A Horse Named Bailey

As she sits astride his broad, strong back
And pats his head so erect and proud
She can sense his excitement, for he wants to be off
He is not at all daunted by the crowd

His coat lovingly brushed to a velvet sheen
Saddle and reins pliant and smooth
Spectators admiring his bearing and form
As at last she gets the signal to move

Together they take each hurdle and test
He responds to each touch of her knees
His ears prick up as the audience applauds
But she knows that it is her that he's trying to please

The many hours they have trained together
The love that she gave him he has now returned
And as they finally cross the finish line
She realises something they both have learned

That they have both relied on one another
Since they first met, oh so long ago
And the proof of Bailey's love for her
Is the rosette and the trophy won at this year's show.

Don Woods

Angel's Purr

Angel's purr,
Is like a warm, crackling, homely fire.
Causing my rose heart to bloom, cheerier,
And does uplift and comfort me peacefully like life's toiling mire.
His purring *miaow* flutters about me like a summertime butterfly.
Together in hover bird winging love, smouldering in cuddly, furry, fluffy unity
We live our lives by on by on by,
He's my purring feline baby,
I am his adopted daddy.
Two companions.
Purring and, in relief, heating my feet's osteoarthritis
Together in loving unity a pride of purring, simmering African lions.
Such a purring angel.
So purring soft with me and gentle.
With his bushy, hairy, tickly tail and there is a tale.
A touching angelical purr rrr rr r.
Purr rrr rr r.
Purr rrr rr r.

Keith Newing

Fluffers
(May 2002 - September 2009)

Is it worth it?
Time and money
Not just wasted?
They asked

Is it worth it?
There is no future
It is not a child
They said

You were worth
A heart of gold;
Time of my life
I say

You were worth
And you were joy;
Chasing warm sunrays
To play

My friend in the hay
Love you forever
And a day
You are worth it!

Birgit Ianniello

Cat

Sit, stay
And
Sleep
Like a child
In a certain way.
A deep
Knowing smile
To keep
You content
And then
The realisation
Of a moment,
And again.
Silence again.

Nicola Barnes

Spider Spinstress

She watches me from the corner of the bathroom,
Beady eyes as irritated as an old headmistress
Finding an unruly me at fourteen in unlawful place,
With a *what do you want, I'm rather busy* feel to it.
She is. She's the biggest Lady Longlegs I've ever met
And the busiest. I sidle into the room, duster in hand,
Behind my back, so as not to offend, but she sashays
Down, light as air, her chiffon curtains swaying,
And I lose heart and retreat. One morning, I know,
We will wake, completely enveloped in steel gossamer,
Totally cocooned in her funereal winding sheets,
But for now she's busy creating a fantasy outfit
Fit for Lady Gaga's next appearance.
I must not delay her.

Liz Davies

Today I Heard The Dog Whimpering

Today it was a gentle whimpering sound
Which touched my heart
I wanted to put my hands over my ears
Why won't someone talk to the dog?
Day after day sitting in his large kennel
At the end of the garden
Usually he barks and barks and barks
Why do they never hear him?
I feel that when he is desperate
Too tired to bark anymore,
He then whimpers and that hurts me so much
So much more than all the barking
He sounds so sad, dejected and alone.

How can you explain to a dog
The owners never hear his distress
They never scold him for barking
It is the silence from them
That is so terrible, day after day,
I'll hear him and want to set him free
I want to let him loose
I want to make him feel better
Stroke him, hug him, walk him,
Show him love and care
Tell him what a good and patient dog he is.
Every day for the moments I am here
I can't let that sound go.

Here in Montenegro they would not
Understand my feelings and fears
This is the way it is or can be
For his life perhaps it is better
Than all the stray dogs on the streets
Careful how you speak to a stray dog,
Show kindness, touch them, give them titbits
If you get too close to them
They will follow you everywhere
That would be so unkind,
Heart wrenching. Wagging tails,
Doleful, pleading eyes
Please take me home.

On one occasion an old dog
Just able to walk
Hungry, longing for a home
Lunged into the back of our car
Cowering down behind the back seat
Pleading with his eyes *please*
Take me home. It was so painful
So difficult to get him out of the car
So emotional leaving him on the roadside
Every day somewhere, everywhere
Dogs watch you, scared of you
They wag their tails but cower or run
They know people can, first coax then kick.

Some people can be kind
What a life, when a dog never knows.
Most days at some point my heart
Misses a beat watching dogs limping,
Legs bent, possibly broken at some time,
Shuffling down the roads.
Am I letting all the dogs down
By taking no action?
Then what about the seals?
The elephants? The turtles? Ethiopia?
Prisoners of conscience
Where do our feelings stop?
Where do our actions start?
And will they?

I hear the whimpering from next door
Stifling an urge to grab the dog and run
I go inside and put the music on
I start to prepare lunch
Then in conversation I say to my husband
'The dog was whimpering again today'
He looks at me and says
'You worry far too much for everyone'
I smile at him and nod
For most of my life I have wanted so much
To take the pain for others
That is not possible *but*
Tomorrow will be another day!

Susie Sullivan

Shelley

One day I got a little kitten
A tabby, six weeks old
I fetched her from round the corner
Away from her mother's fold
I decided to call her Shelley
Hewll Bennett played him you know
I really did fancy him
But Shel did not look like him though
Shelley was very friendly
Particularly with my dad
Following him around the garden
Sometimes running as if he were mad.
When Mum and Dad went on holiday
He was always a very good friend
Always at the gate to meet me
When a day's work came to an end
But after nine years Shelley took sick
Bad news, soon we knew
Shelley had got leukaemia
Putting her down was the kind thing to do
The day she was due at the vets
There was sadness all round the place
I hugged her and thanked her for nine happy years
And wished her luck in a more holy place
I ran out of the door to work
Not wishing Mum and Dad to see my tears
Then Mum shouted 'Fasten your coat'
A mother's love never disappears
I walked feeling full of grief
That my tears were about to erupt
Then I met one of Dad's friends
And his chatter helped cheer me up
Shelley has gone to a better place
But how I miss that Shelley cat
People say get yourself another
But Shelley's irreplaceable and that's that.

Jenny Bosworth

Motherhood
(Smokey, our loyal feline friend)

Fluffy and slinky, shiny and neat
Her fur is soft and body petite,
Purring and grooming from head to tail
Paying attention to every detail.

Next she yawns and gives a stretch
Her kittens now she will fetch,
They play by an open door
A perfect litter totalling four.

Proudly she washes as she feeds
Seeing each kitten has all it needs,
No better mother could there be
Than those that to their babies see.

In the basket each one she places
Safe from harm and all our faces,
Lying there now like balls of silk
Now mother rests and drinks some milk.

Elizabeth Murray-Shipley

Brilliant Tom

I seldom wonder why my cat Tom is so fat,
It's because his breakfast is a fat bush rat.
My daughter Rachel named him Fat Man,
Because he loves to scratch for food in her baking pan.
Fat Man is like a ghost at night,
His eyes are like a brilliant torch light . . .
He jumps over the moonlit streams,
And climbs on top of a tree to rest and dream.
My daughter Rachel feeds him every day,
And laughs at him when he meditates and pray.
He would close his eyes and fold his paws,
And suddenly scratches at his victims with his deadly claws.
At times I wonder why he sleeps on a big mat,
And plays a prank as if he is dead for the rats.
He beats his big fat fluffy tail and watches TV,
He enjoys Tom and Jerry and said, 'That's me!'
My son Daniel will cuddle Tom in his hands,
He sings to him that's all he understands.
Tom is a lover of great music I am told,
He shakes his waist and dances in winter's cold.
Tom fell in love with his neighbour's cat Mary,
My daughter tells me it's time for Tom to marry.
At nights he will call for Mary in the grass,
Then Mary will cry and show up at last.
What a romantic couple these two can be,
They romanced each other and rejoiced happily.
My lovely cat Tom wears a robe in the cold,
He is so beautiful for my eyes to behold.
He climbs the flower trees to sway and dance,
And waits for the lizards when he has a chance.
His brown and white velvet back is what I admire,
What a magnificent pet my heart desires!
He eats his bread soaked in milk and milo,
And licks his paws when he eats ghello.
He walks like a tiger and shakes his waist,
And pounces on his prey in elegance and grace.
Tom captivates my children every day,
They took him to church one day to watch him pray.
Tom is my brilliant cat I called Fat Man,
Because he loves to lick at my frying pan.

Cecil Gideon

Animal Antics 2012

Forward Poetry Information

We hope you have enjoyed reading this book - and that you will continue to enjoy it in the coming years.

If you like reading and writing poetry drop us a line, or give us a call, and we'll send you a free information pack.

Alternatively if you would like to order further copies of this book or any of our other titles, then please give us a call or log onto our website at www.forwardpoetry.co.uk

Forward Poetry Information
Remus House
Coltsfoot Drive
Peterborough
PE2 9BF
(01733) 890099